KEEPING
SECRETS

. . . .

The White House, the Military and
Business Leaks that Threaten our
National Security

. . . .

By

DENNIS F. POINDEXTER

TABLE OF CONTENTS

PREFACE

Secrets in the News

In his introduction to *Open Secrets, Wikileaks, War and American Diplomacy,* Bill Keller wrote of the New York Times engagement with Julian Assange before the publication on the Internet of a series of classified State Department documents. One of the attorneys for the mercurial leader of Wikileaks, sent out a mock Christmas card that said:

> "Dear Kids,
> Santa is Mum and Dad,
> Love,
> Wikileaks"[1]

This summarizes the types of secrets we deal with every day. The formal kind that Wikileaks posted on their website were government secrets, still clearly marked as SECRET, so we can tell they are important. When the Federal government makes a secret, we can usually tell it was intended to be one.

At the same time, we deal with many other kinds of things, from the formula for Coca-Cola, to the idea that Santa was not really putting those great gifts under the tree. Some of those things are not so easy to define as secrets, and keeping them is much more complicated.

---

1   *Open Secrets, Wikileaks, War and American Diplomacy* (Grove Press, New York, New York), Page 22.

No secret is forever. This is not a good reason to let them out in the public, but it is something that we should consider when making them. We should run our lives with the knowledge that any secret we have will eventually be known to many, who we might think, should not know it. Of course, we don't run our lives that way, so it comes as a surprise that a thing we held close was bouncing around on someone's Facebook page, for everyone to see. There are consequences to ignoring the loss of secrets and, generally, the bigger the secret, the more the damage from the loss of it.

We seem to have not developed a good value proposition for secrets, so "bigger" is not so easy to define. We pretend we have this down to a science and can risk manage almost anything, presenting colorful slides and graphs that are testimony to our ability to predict what will happen in the future. When one paragraph of a note, sent from one employee to another, is the smoking gun that leads to a $25 Billion settlement, "bigger" takes on a new meaning.

It is not fair to the keeper of a secret to have someone else tell it to the whole of the free world. It is hard and unrewarding work to keep a secret when the keeper discovers everyone already knows. Yet, the White House tells a secret that the Intelligence Community will keep, almost forever. We need a new definition of secret to fit something that everyone knows.

Christmas

On December 25, 2009, Umar Farouk Abdulmutallab, who probably has the least spell able name of any terrorist ever, tried to blow up an airplane coming into Detroit, the TV news was full of stories about bad guys and the secret things we did to catch them. Certainly the fact that he did try to blow up an airplane was not a secret because everyone on the plane was sure to know that smoke was coming from his underwear and not the cart the attendants were pushing up and down the isle, and quite a bit of yelling and screaming accompanied the detention of this person. This was not a secret to anyone.

It was probably not even a secret that he was a terrorist, since not very many people other than the shoe bomber have ever tried to set themselves on fire on an airplane. So, even though these two would-be bombers are not the ones that spring into my mind at the sound of the word "Terrorist", we all know they are. The tricky area of who is a terrorist, and who is a patriot, makes this more difficult to decide, but we generally know one, when we see one.

The real secret, which we can call a Really Big Secret, to distinguish it from other run-of-the-mill secrets, was the announcement on ABC News that Abdulmutallab had been making phone calls from overseas and those phone calls were twice monitored by NSA, (The National Security Agency to people who have never heard of them before). ABC said NSA told other people in the government that Abdulmutallab was worth watching. The source of this, surprisingly, was the White House Counterterrorism Advisor. Perhaps it was not a secret, after all. Indeed, NSA themselves had made a press release on the very same subject, so it is not likely that the fact that NSA monitors people on their phones was any Really Big Secret, but if you go to their website you will not see anything about monitoring anyone, anywhere. Besides, anyone who has experience with NSA, knows they are not very good about answering questions about this type of thing, or anything else for that matter. We always called NSA, "Never Say Anything" and it was not a compliment about their way of keeping secrets.

In 2001, the post-9/11 cleansing resulted in almost everything involved with tracking terrorists being investigated at least three times. One of the things coming out of the Congressional side of the inquiries was that NSA had monitored three of the hijackers and knew they were up to something. Twelve years ago, that was big news. They passed this information along to the CIA. CIA then found out they were coming to the U.S. Nobody said anything to the FBI, leaving the question of whether the FBI would have or could have done anything if they had known. [2] This brought out the whole issue of information sharing, prompting the Intelligence Agencies to set off a set of "information sharing initiatives" to help the agencies cooperate better. Public reporting of this started in 2009 with the declassification of some of the material written during the post 9-11 Congressional inquiries, making it clear that NSA did indeed monitor the phone calls of people who were, or might become, terrorists. After all the mudslinging and finger-pointing was over, the agencies were gun-shy about having these types of accusations made again, and the Really Big Secret of NSA monitoring of the cell phones of terrorists was out. It had been out plenty of times before, in books and articles by various people, but this time, the government was confirming it. Most governments know better.

Now, we know terrorists' cell phones were being monitored, and we were using that monitoring to kill some of them. In a series of lengthy articles about the President's views of the near disaster in Detroit, the New York Times said the result was a renewed effort to sharpen the list of potential targets of U.S. drone strikes and put himself in the position of having the last say in whether or not a terrorist was to be killed by a missile from the sky. A few people, who didn't know we were using airborne drones to attack people, may have thought the Army had developed the perfect robotic soldier, but the vast majority of us knew what drones these articles were talking about. We can see the different kinds of them on the Internet. They are not a secret.

It looked like we going to try to kill some of these terrorists before they could put another underwear bomber on a plane. That seemed like a good idea, and that may not have been a secret since half the world says they are going to kill people who attack them and none of us think anything about it. We expect that kind of reaction.

While the legal beagles publically debate the ethical, moral and legal issues that surround a person who can make the decision to kill a U.S. citizen in another country[3], I was glad somebody was doing it and didn't much care if he was going to attack a few people in Yemen whether they were U.S. citizens, or not. They were not over there on tourist visas and the President, who knows international law, probably knew what he was doing. Whoever was talking about this to the press didn't.

The sources for these stories are not mentioned, except as "two officials present", which kind of narrows it down, unless there was a room full of people there that day. They probably have records on who attended their meeting, since governments almost always keep records of everything a person might be blamed for. If they look, they will find out who leaked the information. They must not be looking because the list is not that long.

In a follow-on article the Times put together a summary citing several administration officials on Obama's counter terrorism record. In this article, they named some of the people they had interviewed about what is a set of some of our Really Big Secrets concerned with how President Obama directs the efforts to kill some of our least accessible enemies in Al Qaeda:

Senator Saxby Chambliss, Republican of Georgia and the vice chairman of the Senate Intelligence Committee "We've crippled Al Qaeda. The foundation may have been laid in the Bush administration, but you have to recognize that this administration has been very committed to carrying the fight to the enemy."

William M. Daley, President Obama's chief of staff in 2011, said the president has frequently remarked that "nothing comes to me that's easy to decide," and has been frustrated by an inability sometimes to get real-time information when strikes appeared to have gone awry…

General James. L. Jones, the national security adviser from January 2009-November 2010, on how over time President Obama grew more comfortable with the drone program: '...He certainly adopted a principle of leadership that I absolutely agree with — that if you're going to be blamed for something if it goes wrong, you want to understand what it is you're agreeing to when you say yes.'

Dennis C. Blair, former Director of National Intelligence, on what remains to be done: '...I'm all for drone strikes if there's no downside. But in this case there's a huge downside — we are making it more difficult for governments and Muslims that can cooperate with us against Al Qaeda to do so...'

Antony J. Blinken, national security adviser to Vice President Joseph R. Biden Jr. on how the President was responsible for many of the difficult decisions that had to be made. [4]

Of course there were probably more sources that were not named, but they weren't talking about those. Some sources like to be anonymous. Those are usually the "sources requesting they be anonymous because they are not authorized to speak on the sensitive subject." Most people, who are not authorized to speak on the subject, should not be doing that, but they do anyway. Some people like to be named so they can play their own Game of Thrones. Some people don't like to be named, because they know what a dangerous game this is.

---

2   The 9/11 Commission Report: Identifying and Preventing Terrorist Financing, 23 August 2004

3   Joe Becker and Scott Shane, *Assessing Obama's Counterterrorism Record*, New York Times, 29 May 2012, accessed 6 Nov 2012, http://www.nytimes.com/2012/05/29/world/obamas-leadership-in-war-on-al-qaeda.html?pagewanted=all and Secret 'Kill List' Proves a Test of Obama's Principles and Will, 29 May 2012, accessed 6 Nov 2012. http://www.nytimes.com/2012/05/29/world/assessing-obamas-counterterrorism-record.html?_r=1

4   Ibid, Joe Becker and Scott Shane

CHAPTER 1

When the President Makes a Secret

The hard question is whether the information about the clandestine program was leaked to the press with the sole intent of making the President of the United States look good. Senator McCain, from the Senate floor, accused the administration of doing that. Generally speaking, this blunt approach isn't used very often in Washington, but the good Senator can do what he wants, protocols or not.

He was right about one thing; these types of programs always end up in the President's lap, one way or another. Only the President has the legal authority to approve them. It is his job, and it goes with the territory. You have heard the word "finding" mentioned in all of this and it has a meaning that goes beyond a discovery of something or another. The President has to sign a *finding* to get a program started because that is how covert action programs work. He will know what he is signing because there are lawyers lined up on the hallways of the White House and Congress who will help him decide. Many a government official has tried to launch a program on his own, only to discover that doing this type of thing requires more than just having the idea and coming up with the money to do it. All of a sudden, some General or Admiral finds out he needs a signature to get this going and, by the way, it is going to be something signed by the President. Findings are not trivial things to get, as anyone who ever tried to get a President to sign something will tell you.

There are procedures to getting a finding signed[5]. They require that the finding be in writing, or be put in writing with 48 hours after the decision has been made. Second, it cannot authorize a covert action that has already been made. Third, everyone in any agency will be under the rules and policies of the Central Intelligence Agency. And, a finding may not violate the Constitution or any statute of the United States. That last part is harder to determine on the spur of the moment, but everyone tries to keep a neutral perspective.

It is one of the reasons why every President ends up with grey hair. The number and types of the programs the U.S. can execute is not something the President knows when he gets to the White House. That is because they are Really Big Secrets and not very many people know about them. Even the drone campaign is not the Biggest of the Big, but it is big enough that it shouldn't be the subject of an article in any newspaper. A whole series of investigations of "leaks" is about to get started and when it is over, it will be the most current of a long list of them. As a government, we leak everywhere, and it is not even a new thing, but we should hope they weren't leaks about covert programs. They are the most secret of our secrets. This year, we saw a few leak out.

How Covert is Covert?

Our government has rules about how secrets are protected and they are frequently criticized for all the wrong reasons. At the extremes, we have some super-sensitive things in the classified world of the Intelligence Community that are very well protected and don't get shared with anyone, even if the sharing would be good all around. Some of those have never been seen in the press. Not ever, not any aspect, not a single thing has ever been said about them. Those are secrets that everyone keeps quiet about. Since it is hard to prove that there are such things without naming them, some people would say this is just speculation on my part, but there are plenty of examples of them after the programs were discovered.

In 1986, Ronald Pelton who worked at NSA was convicted of five counts of espionage for selling secrets to the Russians. What followed was a collision of reporters trying to find out what the spying was all about, and the CIA and NSA trying to limit the amount of damage that would come from discussing them in public. NBC published a report saying the United States had submarines collecting intelligence in Russian harbors.[6] That probably was not a big surprise to the Russians, but hearing us admit it probably was. Years later, in *Blind Man's Bluff*, we get details of these little missions into Soviet waters, that included following Russian submarines and tapping into underwater cables[7]. These are definitely not the kind of things an intelligence agency wants to see in the public. They are covert operations. We almost have to ask ourselves what *covert* means if everyone is talking about these programs.

Covert, by definition, means secret. Things that appear in public, like on the Internet or in newspapers, are not secret. But, we can talk about things that are covert, and the programs we talk about will still be secret. This is what I call the Paradox of Secrets.

When I was working in covert programs, we didn't have any such concept, so we didn't talk about them. We thought it was a bad idea. As it turns out, it was just those of us working in covert programs that thought this way. Everyone else, including some officials in the White House, had a different idea. They thought it was OK to talk about covert programs as long as they could just say it was "an unnamed source" or an "Administration representative speaking on the condition of anonymity".

The National Security Act, Section 503, says something covert is "An activity or activities of the United States Government to influence political, economic, or military conditions abroad, where it is intended that the role of the United States Government will not be apparent or acknowledged publicly. ... Covert action encompasses a broad spectrum of activities, but may include:

Propaganda: Intelligence agencies covertly disseminate specific information to advance foreign policy goals. United States law prohibits, however, the use of intelligence agencies to influence domestic media and opinion.

Political/Economic Action: Intelligence agencies covertly influence the political or economic workings of a foreign nation.

Paramilitary Operations: Intelligence agencies covertly train and equip personnel to attack an adversary or to conduct intelligence operations. These operations normally do not involve the use of uniformed military personnel as combatants.

Lethal Action: During times of war or armed conflict, the U.S. may need to use covert lethal force against enemies who pose a threat. The U.S. formally banned the use of political assassinations in 1976 "[5], but this is the kind of thing that drone strikes fall under. Drone strikes are lethal.

One distinction between covert action and other overt activities, such as traditional diplomatic or military operations, is that U.S. officials could plausibly deny involvement in the activity. This "plausible deniability," however, is predicated upon the covert action remaining secret."[8] This is not as simple as it sounds.

This is the kind of thing that Churchill faced in WWII when he decided to let the Germans bomb Coventry rather than sending up Britain's fighters. The Germans could figure out that the Allies had deciphered their encryption codes. The whole idea of how and when we might crack some other country's codes is usually covert. We forget that there are such secrets and they are worth letting someone die for them. I call these Really Big Secrets to distinguish them from run-of-the-mill secrets. They are usually some really special things that our government can do that nobody else in the world knows about.

Years ago, people used to speculate about the ability of some person to do astral projection of their minds to other places of the world and see what was going on. At a dinner, I sat next to a woman who said she could do this and it was hard for me to think about chicken when my brain was thinking about ways to move my seat without being noticed. But, if people were really able to do it, we would not want anyone in the world to know about it. She certainly would not have been talking to anyone about it at dinner; there would not be any background briefings on it at the White House. If it were really covert, I might not know there was such a thing as astral projection, and might never have heard the term.

We would compartment something like this, i.e. divide it into pieces so that only a few people who knew about it had any idea what the whole thing looked like. Some people call this "Above Top Secret" but the government calls it Sensitive Compartmented Information (SCI). Information in these programs is divided up into sections so that nobody can see the whole thing. If someone were to lose part of the information, or somebody steals it, they will not have all the details of the whole. Let's say, for example, that I am building a new ship that can fly. This would be a Really Big Secret that the Chinese would want to know. In case the Chinese, who we know are really good at stealing things from us, got some of the things related to Ships that Fly, they probably could not get everything.

While they are doing intelligence collection, the Chinese discover that that the main thing about the new thing we are building is its ability to fly. Then, they discover that part of the ability

5

to fly is being developed in a warehouse on a dock in San Diego. They conclude that it is probably an airplane that can takeoff and land on water, but this is hardly advanced research since there have been several of those over the years. They think they need to look harder, because they also know the funding for this is coming out of an Advanced Research budget item. Parts of that are available in the published parts of the Defense budget and sometimes from a Congressman who has a constituent with a new line of business to be supported. At some point the Chinese find out that almost everyone on the program has experience with ships, not airplanes, and they go back to the Intelligence drawing board. A year or so later, they see a video from a cell phone that shows a small model ship flying and landing back on the water. The Chinese equivalent of OMG is Twittered all over the place.

Half of the world watches communications of other countries so they see the Chinese sending OMG messages to all their friends but we don't know why they are doing it. This starts the Twitter lines humming all over, trying to see what they are up to. The Chinese don't want us to know that they know anything about it, so they so they divide what they know into three compartments, Ships With Special Capabilities, Things Other than Airplanes That Fly, and the Sources of Information About Ships, maybe who gave them the video, to begin with, or how they managed to get it. There are quite a few compartments that build up, as people hide things from one another. This is why a guy like Aldrich Ames, the CIA spy, can hurt us so much. He knows all the parts of the compartments. He can tell someone about all of those parts. In real life, this is much more complicated, but when someone says, "Above Top Secret", this is what they are talking about.

Second, all secrets have a life. At some point we are going to take this ship out in the daylight and fly it around to see if it works when the sun is shining. A few more people with cell phones and cameras will see it and the secret might not be quite a big as it was before that. But, there will still be secrets in how we make it fly, and how we steer it while it is in the air, but the fact that it flies is not a secret. But, while that ability to fly will eventually be known, the idea is to keep it secret as long as possible.

We would make sure that nobody ever spoke about it off the record, or on. It would be more important than the formula for Coke, which Coca-Cola managed to keep secret for close to 150 years. For some period of time, we should never hear about those kinds of secrets, but in the World of Secrets, nothing is forever.

When, in July 2012, we hear "breaking news" about the President having secretly ordered the CIA to supply arms to Syrian rebels: "The secret order, referred to as an intelligence "finding," allows for clandestine support by the CIA and other agencies. It was unclear when the president signed the authorization for Syria, but the sources said it was within the past several months."[9] The secret lasts as long as people can keep their mouths shut and, apparently, that is not more than several months.

A reasonable person might think the targeting of terrorists by a Predator or Reaper might be similar, but it isn't quite as clear there. Absolutely everyone, who can read, knows the Predator and Reaper are used to kill terrorists. Those planes are big, and when they fly over Pakistan and Yemen, they are pretty hard to keep secret. When a missile goes off and hits a truck, there are quite a few people who see and hear it. Body parts fly off into buildings and places where people live and they take pictures with a cell phone so their friends can see them. They know who fired it off, because Pakistan and Yemen don't have Predators and Reapers in their military arsenal. The world will be a more interesting place when they do.

The Really Big Secrets are in who is on that target list, how we know they should be on it, and where we think we might start finding them. Those are the covert secrets. When the New York Times says the President was flipping through a bunch of target packages for terrorists, trying to decide which ones should be killed; they are getting close to something that needs to be covert.

What we saw was a lawsuit by The American Civil Liberties Union and the Center for Constitutional Rights, that tried to expose the sources and the decision making of the President when he chooses his targets[10]. This suit was brought by the father of Anwar al-Awlaki, a favorite in the Al Qaeda terrorist organization, and their lead operator in Yemen. The speculation in the article is the U.S. would have to disclose secrets of how it arrived at the conclusion Al-Awlaki was to be killed and justify why he was killed in Yemen. Only in America, can anyone entertain such a thing as this, and maybe not even here, since it didn't get far in the court system.

If a person is not in the White House, it does not appear to make much difference in how they treat secrets. We find that seven members of Seal Team Six, the one that killed Osama Bin Laden, was giving information to the makers of *Medal of Honor: Warfighter*, a video game, so they could make it more realistic, giving tactical and special equipment details to them[11]. For that, they received "non-judicial punishment, which from my days in the Air Force, is a light touch on the wrist, that to a SEAL is not going to hurt their career. They are like gods in the Navy.

On the same day this story was released, the Pentagon released another story about a drone being attacked by Iran, five days before the Presidential election, and everyone managed to keep quiet about it until after the election was over.[12] This little bit of magic was keeping secrets for all the wrong reasons, but they were keeping a few in this single incident, and giving them up later. (You might remember the same criticism raised by Congressional Committees looking into the death of our Ambassador in Libya.)

The article claims we were flying a Predator drone 16 miles from the coast of Iran, (CNN says it was in the Straights of Hormuz).

> "The government's disclosure reveals for the first time a classified U.S. surveillance program."

The Iranians obviously knew it was the U.S., because we are the only ones within a million miles that could claim to have Predator drones. They launched a couple of those Su-25 fighters, which are worthless against other fighters and drones, firing off a few rounds and missing. We could have continued to say nothing, in the same way that we don't advertise or discuss any other kinds of surveillance we might have that would target Iran, but the Pentagon did not.

Somebody also managed to keep secret the affair of Paula Broadwell and General Petraeus, the recent head of the CIA, until after the election, on the grounds that the Justice Department thought it was just like any other criminal case, so they didn't tell the White House about it. This is preposterous, beyond comprehension, and unbelievable. These are all OK in Washington politics, but so seldom as blatant as this particular incident. It smacks of how the Chinese control their press and government officials, than how America the Beautiful operates.

There are times when this kind of release is OK, but there is a National Security reason for it. The reason for the release of something that is classified, is itself classified. It won't be something like, "We would like to keep the President in office and want to make him look good." They are usually something related to how the United States wants to influence perceptions of a world event. A famous case of this was the briefings the Bush Administration did on weapons of mass destruction in Iraq. Colin Powell briefed the United Nations:

> "The material I will present to you comes from a variety of sources. Some are U.S. sources. And some are those of other

countries. Some of the sources are technical, such as intercepted telephone conversations and photos taken by satellites. Other sources are people who have risked their lives to let the world know what Saddam Hussein is really up to."

Almost every human being on the planet is pretty sure this information was wrong, but rightness doesn't enter into this, only perceptions. It may be true that people did risk their lives to get that information, and they actually thought it was true. It may have been true at the time they got it. Perceptions are made by publishing photos and drawings that just a few days before, had been Top Secret. In fact, they are probably still Top Secret somewhere. Almost anyone who saw that briefing came away with the idea that Saddam Hussein had weapons of mass destruction and might use them. Fewer people believe that now, but "fewer" is hard to quantify. For some, facts in evidence do not mean their perceptions have changed.

At the other extreme, governments and businesses have other kinds of secrets that protect them from Congress, competitors, regulators, Boards, and the general public. This class of secrets is bigger, and as important, as some of the government's biggest secrets. I should probably add, just as an aside, there are occasions when leaders confuse the types of secrets that Churchill had to deal with and the type that protects them from external scrutiny. It doesn't always help to have policy to discourage them from hiding things, especially when people just ignore it. Businesses are guilty of the same thing, usually for the same reasons. We should be able to see the difference between classes of secrets that are protected because of some advantage it gives a business or our country, and secrets that protect somebody from critics, but it is hard to tell sometimes.

I use the example of my favorite whistleblower, Thomas Drake, a former CIA analyst and National Security Agency (NSA) manager who tried to take on his bosses at NSA and proved, beyond a shadow of a spy agency, that whistleblowers are not welcome anywhere around Washington. What happened to Drake was an indication that, in spite of the many "Whistleblower Protection" laws that have been made into policy, being a whistleblower is not a protected enterprise. This is worse than being a criminal where you might get a lethal injection. In Washington, they will drag you out in the back, and bury you alive.

Drake was trying to tell his senior managers at NSA, that the software they were working on was not as good as the one his group had put together.[13] This happens all the time in government and business where competing interests for scarce resources dictate the "mine is better than yours" argument. Usually these debates are really about money, which gets enough to continue their projects, and not about the real quality of the software that is created. Seldom does it take a Top Secret report from the Department of Defense to prove anything, one way or another, but this one did. [14]

THINTHREAD was Drake's project and he thought it worked pretty well and offered a cheaper and easier way to do something that is specifically described in a redacted portion a classified Inspector General report, leaving a person to speculate, "NSA enhanced digital network exploitation systems… [in a way that was] "inefficiently using resources" and …"may be developing a less capable long-term digital network exploitation solution that will take longer and cost significantly more to develop." Redactions have always been a mystery to me, but take something poorly written and start redacting it, and this is what you get.

So, it appears, Drake was right about his opinion that THIN-THREAD was a better product, and cheaper than the alternatives. Being right does not usually win out. As my father used to say, "You can be right or you can be loved, so choose carefully." Drake was not loved for his opinions, but what he was really not loved for was his way of getting them out into the public domain. This is where most whistleblowers go wrong.

The Government Accountability Project says "Left with no other options, Drake began legally communicating with a *Baltimore Sun* reporter about Trailblazer – never sharing any classified information…. The *Sun* published a series of articles exposing the $1.2 billion debacle."

This is where "right" gets a little cloudy, since a government employee, with the kinds of security clearances Drake had, cannot give any information to the press without having his work approved for public release. The agreement doesn't say anything about "if you have no other choice". The employee does not get to decide that something is not classified; the government does a review to decide if it is, or isn't. The dilemma for Drake, of course, is allowing the government to review what the author is about to send over to those reporters. Most whistleblowers don't like sending it to anyone to review, and I can't blame them. Nobody in his right mind will approve the release of something that makes them look bad, especially something they will then read about in a newspaper.

Probably the best example of secrets in this class is Watergate. There were secrets everywhere in this, and they were a good layering of all the kinds that we see in real life. The Watergate scandal forced President Nixon out of office, though not without an agonizing period of knife-slashing by the press and the White House. They play rough, and cut deep.

The source used to keep the investigation on track was W. Mark Felt and he was, at one time, the number two person in the FBI.[15] The fact that he was retired, and was not compromised as the source from the 1970's until 2005, was a credit to

Bob Woodward, Carl Bernstein and to Felt himself. They kept a source's name from becoming public, and Felt kept his mouth shut. In 2013, Woodward and Bernstein were both on Face the Nation talking to Bob Shieffer and never mentioned their sources. Old habits die hard. The two reporters could have had 20 of them and only mentioned one, so we will never know who they all were. We just know one.

It almost never happens this way because either the reporters say too much about the source, or the source says too much to someone that should be able to be trusted. On rare occasions, reporters go to jail to protect a source, but if I were the source, I wouldn't bet on it. People will eventually talk too much, and the secret will not be one anymore. That usually happens before the person dies.

Watergate demonstrated all there is to know about secrets. Technically, Felt was not a whistleblower, even though he is often thought of as one; he was an *informant* to a pair of newspapermen. He would not have had any protection, and would probably have been taken care of, had the public discovered his identity. People, who do this sort of thing, hardly ever get protection from anyone. In Watergate, it was not just anyone.

Watergate started with an illegal wiretap of the Democratic National Committee Headquarters, conducted with the knowledge of the President of the United States and the Committee to Re-elect the President, a cover-up, denials and lots of drama. It was reported by two young reporters from the Washington Post. It dragged out for a long time, selling a lot of newspapers. Mark Felt did not publish secrets; he confirmed what the two reporters discovered on their own, adding details. Technically, he should not have been doing that either, but something told him he should. Adding excitement to this was the discovery that the conversations of the President's advisors were recorded in the oval office, which was also a secret. Nobody records things in a government office unless they have a death wish.

The FBI certainly had a secret, but this is not unusual. We might have to wonder if anyone there knew that Felt was talking to the press. Government agencies keep secrets from each other all the time, and sometimes it is justified. It would not have been difficult to figure out what would have happened to Mr. Felt if the White House had discovered his identity, so either nobody did, or nobody told the White House if they did. This is the particularly dangerous Washington Politics and it is like being a gunfighter in the old West. If you were really good, you might live, but you could still be shot in the back by someone and never see it coming. It is an adventure.

He was, of course, worried about being wiretapped, since the White House did not seem to mind that it was illegal. They probably could have found a good reason to do it legally anyway, so that didn't matter very much. In these days of electronic communications, there is almost nothing that isn't monitored by someone somewhere, and it would not have to be our Federal Government doing it. It might be somebody else's government. Every country has their NSA that monitors those telephone calls, so we might guess that on any given day, everyone in the world is being monitored by someone, and probably more than one someone. They are all looking for somebody else's secrets.

It would be quite a secret for anyone to know, and you can bet there were a lot of people in the world's Intelligence agencies who were looking. A few countries were certainly following what was going on and had their own sources of information about what was happening. They just didn't tell anyone what they found out. We keep a number of secrets that all of our enemies know.

The FBI has a few formal secrets that it keeps about wiretapping in the U.S., since they are the ones authorized to do it.

The White House tried to get the CIA to call off the FBI investigation into the break-in, using national security grounds as the reason. This is a misuse of the classification system but they would have not been a speed bump to anyone involved in breaking into the Democratic National Convention Headquarters. Many Federal agencies have used the "National Security" get-out-of-jail-free card to head off embarrassing themselves, and these guys were no different. I have trouble believing that anyone would take this seriously, even back then, but once the panic sets in, believability goes out the window. They pretend they believe it.

The FBI apparently believed the CIA might have done the break-in and suspected a link between the Bay of Pigs, in Cuba, and this case. The White House could have classified this relationship and said it was a National Security secret. This almost seems bizarre now, after all these years, but think about the logic of it.

People in the FBI actually had to believe that the CIA would conduct a break-in at the Democratic National Convention Offices. Making it easier to believe was a response by one of the burglars [James McChord] who was asked where he was employed said something about "the CIA". He had retired from the CIA in 1970, two years before the break-in. People who actually work for the CIA do not say so. The police, and any child on the street in Washington D.C., know this, but somehow they thought this guy might be working for The Agency. One of the Washington Post reporters there thought it was worth looking into.

People in the White House thought they could convince the CIA to talk to the FBI about calling off the investigation. This really seems funny to anyone who has ever worked for these agencies, but people in the White House usually don't think about how government agencies get along. The CIA was not going to touch anything related to domestic spying, so somebody over there was probably saying, "I'm sorry; you seem to have the wrong number" to any calls they got from the Bureau.

The FBI might have had more than one investigation going on, although I'm not sure why they wanted to investigate a break-in at the DNC, which seems to be a local police matter. Eventually, they would need to try to figure out who Deep Throat was, and that would have been a secret. The White House could have been investigating that one too. Investigations can be both formal secrets and political secrets at the same time, when they are classified. So, we have a mix of both kinds here, the Top Secret kind and the "Friends of Nixon" kind. There were also investigations by a Special Prosecutor's office and the Senate Watergate Committee. These are very complicated layers of secrets that are controlled by various groups and there are so many it is hard to keep track of all of them.

In spite of that, every day, in the Washington Post, there were new articles about what might have happened at those meetings. Quite a bit of that was gossip and secrets of various people in government. These are called "leaks" or "releases" depending on which side the information comes from. Since these were being printed in a newspaper, if they followed their training, nobody with a security clearance could confirm or deny them. This really means that nobody like Mr. Felt can tell the reporters that they are on the right track, because that means confirming something that they know to be a secret. That was really what Felt was doing with the Washington Post reporters.

Our training used to say that, even if you were sure what a press report was saying was not true, you should not tell anyone at the newspaper because just doing that would give out new information that might be classified. This is a little hard to determine sometimes, and not always will it have a yes or no answer. I always stayed away from the press and kept things simple.

The story would have died in 1972, had nobody confirmed anything to anyone. To those of us that were around then, we saw what happened when it didn't. We got to watch President Nixon walk up that helicopter on the White House lawn and wave as he left after resigning. For the younger people, this is just history that the schools never got to, but he actually did resign from office.

What makes it hard for people with secrets, is we talk about them all the time. The *Paradox of Secrets* allows us some leeway in talking about things that are secret, but there are two problems with the practice. First, some companies and government agencies will maintain the secrecy of something long after it is well known and, second, after it needs protection. The leak investigations surrounding the White House of 2012 will only be scratching the surface of what has been leaked intentionally, or by accident, yet we continue to protect things that were no longer secrets, by any definition. Everyone knows about them.

For the White House to release the information about the monitoring of Abdulmutallab, it intentionally gave out things that will be releasable to the public. They send out press releases or hand them out at the Press Room. Anything we give the press is public, even if it is with the understanding that we are not authorized to speak about it because it is sensitive. Under government rules, the things the White House gave out have to be *unclassified* and consistent with policy. It would be hard for NSA, or anyone else, to say it wasn't, unless they challenge the oval office on the classification markings. Government Agencies with suicidal tendencies might do this, but nobody else would.

In the end, how you feel about the protection of secrets will govern how you feel about the outcome of Watergate. If you believe that secrets need to be kept, no matter what, then the outcome would have been different. If you believe that some secrets are made to protect misconduct, then you might be more tolerant of what Deep Throat was trying to do. It is not an easy call, either way, but keeping secrets is not either.

---

5   50 USC § 413B - PRESIDENTIAL APPROVAL AND REPORTING OF COVERT ACTIONS

6   James O'Shea and George Curry, *CIA's Shot at Media Backfires*, Chicago Tribune, June 01, 1986 http://articles.chicagotribune.com/1986-06-01/news/8602080783_1_pelton-trial-ronald-pelton-pelton-case

7   Sherry Sontag, Christopher Drew, *Blind Man's Bluff*, Harper Collins Publisher (New York, New York), page 416.

8   Aki J. Peritz, Eric Rosenbach, Published as a background memo in Confrontation or Collaboration Congress and the Intelligence Community, Belfer Center for Science and International Affairs, John F. Kennedy School of Government, Harvard University, July 2009, http://belfercenter.ksg.harvard.edu/publication/19149/covert_action.html

9   Elise Labott, *Obama Authorized Covert Support for Syrian Rebels*, Sources Say, CNN, August 1, 2012 http://www.cnn.com/2012/08/01/us/syria-rebels-us-aid/index.html

10   Siobhan Gorman, *Drone Victims' Kin Sue Government*, Wall Street Journal, July 18, 2012 http://online.wsj.com/article/SB10000872396390444097904577535321940484032.html

11   Associated Press, *Seven Navy SEALS Reprimanded for Leaking Information*, 8 November 2012, Wall Street Journal, accessed 9 November. http://online.wsj.com/article/SB10001424127887324439804578107921717194356.html

12   Julian Barnes & Jay Solomon, *Iran Fired on U.S. Drone before Vote*, Wall Street Journal, 9 November 2012, http://online.wsj.com/article/SB10001424127887324439804578107191429662874.html

13   See a detailed view at the Government Accountability Project, NSA Whistleblower Thomas Drake (http://whistleblower.org/action-center/save-tom-drake)

14   Department of Defense Inspector General, *Requirements for the TRAILBLAZER and THINTHREAD Systems* (redacted), December 15, 2004 [Note: redacted here means there are one or two lines of text on a printed page and not much more]. http://www.fas.org/irp/agency/dod/ig-thinthread.pdf

15   David Von Drehle FBI's No. 2 Was 'Deep Throat', Mark Felt Ends 30-Year Mystery of The Post's Watergate Source, Washington Post, 1 June 2005. http://www.washingtonpost.com/wp-dyn/content/article/2005/05/31/AR2005053100655.html and a very good summary report of the whole Watergate saga is at http://www.washingtonpost.com/wp-srv/politics/special/watergate/part2.html

CHAPTER 2

When a Country Has a Secret

Like businesses, countries are interested in protecting themselves from the competition. Some of them are open about it and declare what they are doing to keep their competitive advantage; some are liars and thieves trying to pretend to be good world citizens. On most days, there will be some evidence of each kind for almost any country. It is hard to not be skeptical about what is said in public. You find the same kind of thing in office relationships and business arrangements, only the consequences are a little greater here.

When countries protect their National Security interests, they spy on each other, so they have reason to limit what they say about that kind of activity. Things that are not secrets can be found easily enough, but every country steals secrets from everyone they can – friends and allies, or enemies. They steal almost anything they can and sort it out afterwards by analyzing the data for "threats" to their country. Threats vary according to who is doing the analysis, so what a guard on the Golan Heights collects for Israel, is a threat to the regime in Syria. They will want to protect themselves from that as much as possible and try to get their own information about how much Israel knows. There is work on both sides of this, for every country involved and practical limits to how much of this any country can do.

Since every country steals things from the others, each of them has some kind of security they set up to protect their secrets. It takes time and resources to get secrets out of another country that is working to stop this kind of thing from happening. It isn't possible to steal everything, though the Chinese are certainly trying, so we have to narrow down the list of things we really need to protect our country. We usually shorten the list by saying we have some National Interests that are really important so we will focus on those. The number and types of things that are national interests is broad enough to make sure we have a large commitment to intelligence collection. We can debate whether $80 billion a year is too much or too little, but we are often glad to have the information that comes from it.

Our National interests are "conditions that are strictly necessary to safeguard and enhance Americans' survival and well-being in a free and secure nation" falling into these types of categories:

Extremely important US national interests are to:

1. Prevent, deter, and reduce the threat of the use of nuclear, biological, or chemical weapons anywhere;

2. Prevent the regional proliferation of WMD and delivery systems;

3. Promote the acceptance of international rules of law and mechanisms for resolving or managing disputes peacefully;

4. Prevent the emergence of a regional hegemony in important regions, especially the Persian Gulf;

5. Promote the well-being of US allies and friends and protect them from external aggression;

6. Promote democracy, prosperity, and stability in the Western Hemisphere;

7. Prevent, manage, and, if possible at reasonable cost, end major conflicts in important geographic regions;

8. Maintain a lead in key military-related and other strategic technologies, particularly information systems;

9. Prevent massive, uncontrolled immigration across US borders;

10. Suppress terrorism (especially state-sponsored terrorism), transnational crime, and drug trafficking; and

11. Prevent genocide [16].

Of course there will always be people who will not accept a list like this, but this one was put together by people like Richard Armitage, Robert Ellsworth, David Gergen, Andrew Goodpaster, Bob Graham, John McCain, Sam Nunn, Condoleezza Rice, Brent Scowcroft, and James Thomson, who have a pretty good idea of what is important to security of the U.S. If this list isn't to your liking, there are plenty of opportunities to publish one of your own. But, most of our Really Big Secrets have some connection to one of these categories.

To make national policy that might begin to solve some of these types of complicated issues, every country needs information about other countries and people who live in several countries, like terrorists who move around a lot. They can get some useful information by flying spy satellites around, but that is far from enough. We have to have reports from human beings who have been inside the factory or the underground place where they make those poison gas canisters to be sure of what they are doing and how. Pictures would be nice. Samples would be really nice. Copy a few computer records while you are at it. It's no wonder it is so hard to find a good spy.

I interviewed a person who had been a spy in Russia and he was about as calm a person as I have ever seen. He was relaxed and thoughtful about the work of spying, but as he said, "that was a long time ago" and he was not doing it anymore. He had a gun held to his head for several minutes once, while a military officer tried to figure out if he was going to be shot. The officer finally decided he was the wrong person. Spying is stressful, dangerous work, for the person who does it.

So, we collect quite a bit of information about various places, then, analyze all that raw data to make sense of it. It is prioritized and assumptions made about what has happened or what might happen in the future. When we get a surprise, like the one in the Syria, where thousands of people have mobilized to overthrow their government, people start asking why we didn't predict what was going to happen, given all the collection and analysis that we had been doing. It is a fair question.

Spying is divided into a number of things called "INTS" that are general categories of capabilities to pick up certain types of information. HUMINT, Human Intelligence for example, focuses on information that is collected from human sources. If I interview businessmen who comes from a long stay in China, I would be trying to find out what I can about Chinese operations from the perspective of someone who has worked with them.

With COMINT, I could intercept telephone calls, faxes and e-mails about the same subject. That would give me quite a bit of information, but it wouldn't be of much use without some analysis. I need to know what the how the Chinese work in this area. With MASINT, I can do a spectral analysis of the metal that gadget is made out of. These are all handy things that help make the analysis more accurate. In the absence of this type of technology, persistence works pretty well.

It has to be translated, if not in English, and analyzed. When something happens fast, it takes a couple of days to start to look at some things that were available, and most of the older stuff is not very helpful. Then, something flares up in South America, and we are all wondering why we didn't know it was going to happen. Maybe we should have known. We probably had the information that would lead someone to a conclusion that something was going to happen there, but never got around to looking at it, translating and analyzing it. It can happen.

When countries decide to spy on one another, almost no secret is safe. Some of the bigger ones have resources and capabilities to get any secret they can find, and even a few they didn't know about. Every country steals secrets, but very few do it better than China. They have a long history of espionage, the patience to do it over time, and a pattern of stealing that is inbred in every aspect of their business culture. My last book, The Chinese Information War, covered this subject in greater detail. But, China is not only one country that can affect our national interests.

When I did Industrial Security for the Defense Department, I used to inspect a business, in the western suburbs of Chicago, called Recon Optical. It made special cameras used in high altitude reconnaissance and they were good at it. One government, or another, classified most of the work they did.

In 1986, Israel was caught planning to steal some technology relating to makes those cameras. We see this as National Security Information, which is why we classified it, and Israel saw it as essential to their National Security, a capability they needed to be able to observe their neighbors and enemies. We certainly don't see stealing our secrets as the kind of thing Israel should do for a country that gets $3.1 Billion in military aide every year. It seems like they could afford to buy it. Israel used to buy U.S. companies with that money we gave them, so they could have it both ways. Sometimes they just get careless and in too much of a hurry. We are all like that.

Israel keeps two kinds of intelligence stations, one covert, and one that is recognized; they do this in friendly countries and with their enemies. The Israeli Air Force and El Op Electro-Optics Ltd, apparently worked together to get the plans for certain cameras, and putting an undercover El Op employee into Recon Optical to work there[17]. That sounds like the covert side of their intelligence, but they are deceptive rascals, so it is hard to tell. They shipped out some documents before they were caught stealing them, and were later accused of setting up their own program building similar cameras. If that sounds familiar, it may be because we have had, over the last five years, almost a hundred similar cases and China is behind them all. Israel may steal from us, but it will not keep the President up nights thinking about it. China might.

If we look at the list of critical national interests, it is a little easier to understand why we seem to flop around all over the place looking at different regions of the world. It isn't as disorganized as it may look. We have trouble with Iran and Syria, the rest of the Middle East, Russia, Mexico, Venezuela, and Latin America, all for different reasons. The main concerns are nuclear weapons development in Iran, Syria's civil war with the potential for Weapons of Mass Destruction (WMD), oil supplies and sanctions against Iran, political instability in the Middle East, terrorist expansion into "franchise operations" of Al Qaeda, drug trafficking to the U.S., and uncontrolled immigration. That is how the political situation in Mexico becomes a National Interest.

We have quite a few interests to look out for, each with a set of political decisions that have to be made by the state and National governments. No amount of spying can keep up with the number and diversity of these kinds of goings on, even when we have friends helping us out. We have to prioritize. Three of the things we are concentrating on, besides China, are obvious: Iran, terrorism and WMD. Since Iran is involved in all three of those, a lot of people have to spend time looking at them. Mexico will take a backseat to any of these. This is where secrecy about what we plan to do becomes important. We might agree that Iran is important because it is causing problems with our oil, it supports terror groups, and is looking to build nuclear weapons. These are our highest national security issues. But, finding out what we are going to do about it is to Iran's benefit.

Iran doesn't have a whole lot of friends in the world, but Russia and China have tried to be good neighbors. They keep the UN from passing resolutions that would limit Iran, and their buddies in Syria. Russia and China have tolerated Iran's interest in having nuclear weapons, though why either one of them would want a religiously fanatic, nuclear armed country on their border is a mystery. I can't imagine how we would feel if Mexico were to be taken over by a radical cleric and decided to develop nuclear weapons. We didn't like it very much when the Russians tried to move nuclear-armed missiles into Cuba. We are afraid Iran might try to help some terrorist group, like they are helping the Taliban seeking shelter from those drone strikes in Pakistan. They are going to let them open an office in Iran where they won't have to watch the skies quite so much. It would be easy to give those Taliban a nuke or two just to store for a few years. Worse yet, they are trying to attack targets in the U.S.

Over the years, the Iranians have tried to kill, one way or another, 162 times outside their own borders.[18] Most recently, they have been accused of trying to kill the Saudi ambassador to the United States, Adel al-Jubeir, using Mexican drug gangs to do deed.[19] The person behind the attacks was a representative of Iran's Quds Force, the special-operations unit of the Islamic Revolutionary Guard Corps. An April 2010 Pentagon report shows that Iran's Special Quds Force has an increased presence in Venezuela and support from the government. Hugo Chavez is not one of our favorite people, but he is another one that won't keep the President from losing any sleep, especially now that he is dead.

In 1980, Iran recruited a U.S. convert to Islam to kill Ali Akbar Tabatabai, a former press attaché at the Iranian Embassy in Washington. Ali was a critic of Ayatollah Khomeini and founder of the Iran Freedom Foundation. The recruit killed him and went to Iran where he was never seen again. They are killing, and trying to kill, a good deal more Saudis than U.S. people, by funding regional terrorist groups like Hezbollah to do their work for them.

So, looking at Iran is in the U.S. national interest, and we could hope we get some intelligence that will tell us what they are up to. What we do about Iran – our plans, political positions, and operations – are supposed to be secrets. We have enough trouble with them without having them know what we are doing to counter our moves.

The Iranian government doesn't have to work quite as hard at their spying because they can find out quite a bit about what we know about their tactics, particularly in the Persian Gulf, where the Straits of Hormuz are the choke point for oil passing through to get to markets. Iran deployed submarines, a small flotilla of fast attack boats, and increasing their stock of anti-ship missiles. Iran posts a video of the firing of various short and medium range missiles to prove they can shoot them, but has four missiles climbing into the sky, when only three were launched. It didn't look good for them to have that one left on the launch pad, lifeless, so to speak, so they just added another one.

These are all things we could see easily enough by watching Iran. But an article in the Washington Post[20] says in response to their increased capability, the U.S. Navy is going to deploy the aircraft carrier, USS John C. Stennis to the Gulf four months early so we can maintain two carriers there. They have added new missile defense batteries and radars in Qatar. A Pentagon report says Iran has increased the lethality and effectiveness of their weapons. The

Post article also quoted a report by the Naval War College says the Straights of Hormuz are perfect for the types of tactics used by the Iranian Navy, which should encourage them into all kinds of adventures, if they believe it.

The New York Times reports the U.S. is strengthening its tactical capabilities by moving eight minesweepers into the Gulf. The article says we have increased the number of fighters capable of striking deep into Iran should the situation over the development of nuclear weapons become worse.[21] "Worse" means Israel will try to take out some of the weapon development capability of Iran, which has been moved underground to keep it safe from airstrikes. The Iranians will not be happy about this and start their own version of World War III, a fact later used in an endorsement of Ron Paul for President. A follow-up story by the Times (Elizabeth Bumiller, et al) says the White House is using a secret backchannel of communications to send a message to Ayatollah Khomeini a warning that this was a red line for the U.S. which could drag us into conflict. The Chairman of the Joint Chiefs said on CBS that Iran had the capability to close the Straights. Apparently, we are ready if they do.

The Canadian Press says the HMS Regina has joined a fleet of "a dozen or more warships" operating out of a U.S. base in Bahrain, as a part of Combined Task Force 150, one of three similar task forces operating in the western Indian Ocean.[22]

Are these things that we expect Iran to know, or are they secrets we would not expect them to know? Are they things that can cause us harm if Iran finds out? Yes, and no. The questions have mutually exclusive answers. If they are things that are secrets, they will cause us harm if Iran finds out. If there is backchannel communications with Iran, Iran already knows it but not all the other countries of the world know it. Maybe, Iran doesn't want anyone else knowing it, or even that they are talking to the Great

Satan. If for no other reason than that, it should not be given to a Times reporter to put in a newspaper.

Some of them are things Iran will find out, like when the ships are being deployed. Eventually, they show up over there and they are hard to miss. Iranian spies might even be able to find out when they are leaving port since that is pretty hard to hide too. So, if they will know anyway, it is causing us harm? Yes, it is. They are telling the Iranian government what buildup we are making and when that will start to have an effect on them. When the ships will arrive and how many aircraft are coming are military secrets (not Big Secrets, but they are secrets). Ship movements are classified by the Navy, even though it may only be until the ship gets to its destination.

Our political backchannels are none of the world's business and will definitely do harm. Iran may not be able to use those channels again, or may choose not to, after getting their nose punched over it. What we know about Iran's military capabilities are also secrets, and having those in the press is not good for us. These are not big secrets, but they are secrets that are no longer secret.

I talked to a professor who travelled extensively in China and he was asked why he could not provide answers to certain national security questions. He said, "We are not permitted to discuss national security matters in public." The student said, "Why not? In 100 years we will know it anyway and what good will it have done to have kept it from us?" In 100 years the topic will probably be public knowledge, but right now it isn't. In 100 years all those patented items the Chinese steal will be public knowledge too.

It is the same idea with transient secrets like ship and aircraft deployments. The Iranians will know sometime, so why not now? The trick with this is it isn't an individual decision to make; it is a government decision. The individual who takes the position that one little thing will not matter, is exactly what is getting us into trouble. All those individual decisions, taken together, can tell an enemy quite a bit about us. Iran is an enemy.

An array of Washington and New York journalists and retired government officials speculate on what is happening in Iran and how the U.S. is likely to respond. We, of course, have no idea how much these folks actually know about what we are going to do, but they are on TV. Their speculation does little harm, because it isn't being considered as fact. That might offend some reporters in those cities, but they know that truth is a good defense.

In the middle of all of this comes some things that are new, an Information Warfare attack on Iran's nuclear capability and the assassinations of some of Iran's nuclear scientists. These are much more entertaining than the movement of ships and missiles. This is James Bond's work, for sure.

Viruses, Worms, and .... Death

I had to testify at a hearing once about viruses and worms and found them difficult subjects for judges and juries. You can't see them. They are made out of code that runs in a computer, and the infection process is not like airborne diseases, though some of them sound like they should be. Juries think they understand them if they have anti-virus software on their PC at home. No big deal, they say to themselves; there is a set of virus signatures that these programs look for and, if they see that signature, it gets deleted. Simple.

That part is actually true, since home computer viruses are fairly simple when compared to the types of viruses and worms that governments use against each other. [Just in case you don't have virus software, viruses are attachments to executable code that is passed from one computer to another, usually as an attachment to something, like e-mail. If the code is executed it can do damage to the computer, display unwanted messages, pictures or links to other sites. There are any number of really bad things that viruses can do. A worm can spread without an attachment to the executable, so it is harder to stop and see when dormant. Over the years, these two have blended together and gotten very sophisticated. Several software vendors make their livings keeping up with the new ones and getting rid of them on a computer.]

The class of this software is called *malware,* software that does bad things. People who are in the business of making malware know that there is anti-virus software that will detect it, so they try different things to get around that. They produce variants, new versions that perform better than the old ones; they produce polymorphic viruses that can change, but may be hazardous to their own health; they produce code that executes in memory, but is stored encrypted, so it can't be detected. They are clever and persistent people with too much time on their hands. Software vendors do not do very well at finding and reporting malware before it causes harm to us, even though they try. They are always one step behind the good malware makers. That little window gives the good hackers time to take advantage of a few hundred thousand users before somebody finds "in the wild". Then, it takes more time to fix a solution and get it distributed to people who actually do update their virus signatures regularly.

Most of the time, a few malware makers are hackers trying to make money by stealing banking and credit card information. Governments, being better funded and with even more time on their hands, take this kind of exercise to a new level that can be used for intelligence collection, war, or something better than war.

By now, anyone who follows the news has heard of the Stuxnet worm. In a New York Times article in June of 2012, David Sanger says the President authorized increased cyber attacks, code-named *Olympic Games,* against Iran. These attacks were discussed in the

White House Situation Room with members of the staff and Leon Panetta, Director of CIA, and the Vice President when the Stuxnet worm escaped the confines of the systems it was planted in and got onto the Internet. Each of them is quoted, at length, in the article, giving any reasonable person the idea that Sanger had a source who was there. Before that, it was said to have taken down 1000 or the 5000 centrifuges making nuclear weapons-grade uranium and generally made the Iranians pretty unhappy. This article says, for years the CIA had been introducing faulty parts and designs to slow down the Iranian efforts at building a nuclear weapon.[23] If this isn't James Bond material, I don't know what is.

In order to get into the plant at Natanz, whoever did this had to do what hackers do to map a network; they had to get inside it. A nuclear facility like this would not have a website and e-mail on the Internet. Iran would try to protect its own nuclear secrets. Getting into a network that is closed off from the Internet is harder to do, but the escape of the virus from the Natanz network says it was not as isolated from the Internet as they thought it was. Most networks aren't.

Sanger's article says they got in and planted a beacon, which was inserted using equipment manufactured by Siemens and an Iranian manufacturer. This mapped portions of the network and phoned the National Security Agency to tell them what it had found. Once they knew they could get to the centrifuges, NSA contacted Israel to do the actual work on making a worm to attack it. They used thumb drives to insert it, and it worked (there might have been a hold-your-breath moment in there at the end to bring some suspense into it). Speculation was that Israel was used to let them know that the attack was being successful.

This is a level of detail of a covert program that is never found in public, though Edward Snowden is trying to change that. Somebody in those meetings is idiot enough to provide that kind of detail to at least one member of the press. Sanger gets First Amendment protection from publishing it, but our comparison to Watergate might not hold up very well, unless the White House did try to publish this information with the idea that the President would look good. There is no other reason to tell everyone in the world about this covert program.

The general public does not understand enough about the Stuxnet worm to say, one way or another, but it was far from being a secret. What was secret about it was its connection to the U.S. government.

Two years before this article, most anyone in computer security knew about the worm, what it was doing, how it was doing it, and what countries were affected. An analysis by Symantec, which makes anti-virus software, looked at the attack mechanisms, the development, the spread of the virus in other countries, and had methods of getting it off of computers it had affected.[24] The first discovery of a component of the worm was in November 2008 and there were three variants, each with some changes in the code to make it more effective. The report says Stuxnet was designed to attack controllers of industrial equipment and to keep knowledge of what it was doing from being known by the operators. It described the exact flaws in the systems where it was used that allowed it to spread from one computer to another. The most infected systems were in Iran, Indonesia, and India. [25] Iran said it was not affecting them, even though it was found there. They, apparently, didn't count the thousand or so centrifuges that were damaged.

What nobody knew was where it came from – who originated the thing. Most speculation, including my own, centered around Israel because of a notation in the code to Myrtus, a reference to Esther in the biblical story of Jews overcoming a Persian plot to destroy them.[26] This kind of thing comes from a software guru getting a little too clever, or somebody drawing conclusions from something someone named, without even giving it a thought. It happens all the time because they are so clever, they think they will never get caught. Professionals do not play the game that way. They assume all their efforts will work for a time, but not forever.

Other code analyses went so far as to look at when code changes were made, by time of day and Jewish holidays to draw the same conclusion. The code is posted on-line in several places and can be analyzed by anyone with time to do it. Most of this was speculation, but circumstantial evidence of some involvement of Israel. Stuxnet was not a secret by any means, but most of the world treated it like any other virus or worm. There are thousands of viruses around, they come from many countries, and it takes time to find them and get rid of them. One more, especially one that was not particularly damaging to home or business computers, was not a problem for most users. Most users don't have centrifuges in the basement.

Most of us, in computer security, eventually forgot about Stuxnet because there was a new game in town, *Flame*. Flame spreads in much the same way as Stuxnet because one of its modules is almost identical to a module in Stuxnet, giving rise to the idea that it probably came from the same development environment.[27] It may have been used before Stuxnet, or it may have just had similar dates when it was discovered out in the wild of the Internet. It had been used for at least two years when it was found.

Flame allows remote control that can copy documents, read e-mail and other written notes, record Skype conversations, or record conversations of persons sitting near the computer. In the Intelligence world, this is called Computer Network Exploitation (CNE), referring to the ability to take advantage of vulnerabilities in computer systems to collect some form of information. CNE is always a secret, because it is a two-edged sword. If we can use it, so can someone else. Second, if they know we can use it, they will tighten up their security to keep anyone from doing it again. This makes getting useful information that much harder. The government classifies its CNE to make it harder for other people to find out what they do to get secrets from other countries.

So, if so much is known about Stuxnet and Flame, why should we be concerned at all about the publication of information from the White House? First, if it really was a covert program, that information had to have been Top Secret (and then some) because anytime the President authorizes a covert operation, it needs to be a Really Big Secret. This is something that will cause extremely grave damage to the United States if disclosed to unauthorized people. Internet users, including more than just those reading the New York Times, were certainly not authorized to know about this operation.

The Wired and New York Times articles point to a joint development effort between Israel and the United States to undermine Iran's nuclear development capability. We may be happy that there is such a thing, but it has everyone else in world thinking, "Who is next?" The idea of how such things can be done spreads quickly in the hacker world. It is adapted for use by thousands of people who never thought of it before they saw it. As speculation churns over whether Iran attacked the U.S. banks in September 2012[28] in retaliation for this attack, we may be seeing indications that letting something loose in the world, and leaking the source of it, may have consequences we never anticipated. We should have known better.

Third, it is the first time that U.S. Information Warfare tactics for CNE have been published, while a program was still active, at least that I am aware of. Sanger alludes to an aborted attack, earlier this year, where the White House said it decided not to attack Libya's radars with a virus because the development time would be too long. That kind of thing does not appear in public, because it starts the Libyans and everybody else, looking for viruses in their radars and asking themselves how anyone could get something into a military piece of equipment.

Fourth, anyone with a computer starts thinking that this is a pretty good way to get information from other countries, and they have the code to start working up a new and improved version. We are seeing a lot of imitators, who don't even have to be good coders. They just have to know how to copy it. What's worse, they will probably be using that new code on us. Whoever gave the information to Sanger to write his book, was not trying to help the United States. That could have been intentional, or just stupid, but the result is the same. We are damaged by these disclosures, particularly when they are so detailed.

The Death Star

On November 29, 2010 Majid Shahriari a nuclear scientist at the Shahid Beheshti University, is driving along in rush-hour traffic, with his wife in the car. A Pulsar motorbike rides near the car and the car explodes, killing the scientist and critically injuring his wife. People who live in the Middle East immediately see a connection between the motorbike and the car. Some of us here in the U.S. might have missed it. At almost the same time, another nuclear scientist, also riding with his wife, is nearly killed in the same fashion. In January 2012, Mostafa Ahmadi Roshan, a deputy director of the Natanz nuclear enrichment facility, and his bodyguard, are killed by two individuals who are riding a motorbike and attach a bomb to his Peugeot. The day after a magnetic bomb attached to a motorbike ridden by Massoud Ali-Mohammadi, another Iranian nuclear scientist, kills him. Now, everyone is getting the connection between motorbikes and bombs on cars.

In December, a suspect is arrested based on publication of a Wikileaks document which called the person "a licensed martial arts coach and trainer" writing from Azerbaijan[29]. Majid Jamali Fashi, an Iranian who fits this description is arrested, confesses, and dies by hanging. We know from experience that confessions in some countries are not exactly admissions of guilt, but the Iranians think it is. WIKILEAKS proponents say the release of the diplomatic cable has nothing to do with Fashi's death. It must have been a coincidence. We even have a few reporters saying the same thing.

On August 6, 2012, two men and two women Iranian citizens appeared on Iran's State television to confess to their part in murder. Behzad Abdoli, said he went to Turkey and Cyprus on his way to Israel for fourth-five days of training in riding motorcycles, planting magnetic bombs on moving cars, shooting, taking pictures and personal defense. [30] We have seen this kind of training before, but it is usually some part of Al Qaeda drive by patriotic music and loud explosions shooting fire and debris up into the sky. This time, the person said the training was in a village not far from Tel Aviv.

State television shows eight men and six women who are supposed to be involved in killing some of the nuclear scientists that are part of the same operation that Stuxnet targeted – the Iran nuclear facilities producing weapons grade uranium. Iran had already blamed MI6 in Great Britain, the Mossad in Israel, and the CIA for these murders, though that didn't keep them from hanging Fashi. It sounded like a round-up of the usual suspects, and it probably was. Iran blames these same groups for everything that happens, and if they Stuxnet stories are true, they may be onto something. That is exactly the trouble with telling the world about some of these things.

Now, the truth of who was killing those Iranian nuclear scientists is harder to come by, because half the free world believes that if the U.S. and Israel could work up a plan to infiltrate the computers at the Natanz facility, it is not a far step to believe they might be behind killing those scientists. This is the other problem with leaks. Whether the U.S. has anything to do with it, Iran will say they do, along with MI6. It may be something the Iranians made up, but it doesn't matter to most of the world reading a story about it. The people who really know will not talk and the ones who speculate will give us ten stories to look at. MI6 is looking at this saying, "Where did our name come from?"

I have to say that reporters are partially to blame for what they publish, so not being able to make a court case against one of them for printing something classified does not hold much water here. They know what they are doing, and the responsible journalists will take care in what they publish, even though they don't have a legal requirement to do it. They care about their country enough to be careful. For every ten stories you see in the press, there is another one that you don't see because it was too dangerous to put into print. They can compromise operations that will get our own people killed, or they can compromise sources that end up the same way. In WIKILEAKS releases, the newspapers, particularly the New York Times, argued for withholding some things from the public because it involved sources who might be killed if they were found out. Surely, Mr. Fashi would be glad to know that the system doesn't always work the way it is supposed to. It is a dangerous game to play.

Nobody has said whether the President of the United States looked good because he managed to order the killing of Osama Bin Laden, but is never a very smart thing to do. What makes this dangerous, is the people we are dealing with here. They do not like us very much to begin with. Most leaders try to stay away from looking too good in things like this because it can lead to a tit-for-tat escalation of assassinations like we had in the Cold War. While we may excuse the killing of Osama Bin Laden as an exception, it may have consequences. It is not just a killing that causes this matter to get so much attention. John Brennan, Chief Counterterrorism Advisor to President Obama and Denis McDonough, President Obama's Deputy National Security Advisor briefed Kathryn Bigelow, Academy Award-winning director of *The Hurt Locker*, and screenwriter Mark Boal. They then got to go to the CIA and DoD to visit with people who actually worked on the actual operation.[31] So, not only are they bragging about it, they are helping to make a movie too.

Sometimes, publicity, good or bad, is a dangerous thing. This is why people are trying to exhume the body of Yassir Arafat, who was well known in the Middle East. Arafat was "the most prominent face of Palestinian political opposition to Israel… and the head of the Palestinian Authority." [32]. He was said to have traces of "peculiar" radiation on his clothing, which might mean nothing, or it might mean he was knocked off by an assassination team using something known to that world – polonium 210. Traces of the radioactive substance were found on his clothes, but his autopsy did not show injuries consistent with his exposure. Arab newspapers said he died of torture. The Jerusalem Post said there was no evidence of torture. Other sources said he died of aids or had HIV. The Voice of Russia says the autopsy was inconclusive. Even an autopsy report can be subject to interpretations that are politically motivated.

Two years after Arafat's death there was another death that lead to the purpose behind the autopsy. Alexander Litinenko was a former head of the Russian Federal Security Service, who left Russia after writing a couple of books suggesting Vladimir Putin had come to power because the Secret Police had staged some apartment bombings and terrorist acts that made him look like he was fighting terrorism on the home front. Aside from the idea that this might sound familiar to us, our systems of government are quite a bit different. Not many Russian Premiers would want this kind of thing being said, whether it was true or not, and Litinenko probably knew that. He defected to

Great Britain and was working for the Intelligence Services there, by his wife's account, and died mysteriously in 2006, from what was ultimately determined to be a slow poison. [33] He lost his hair and gradually sank into a physical pit that would not let him out.

Terrorists always want to take credit for killing someone, but governments do not. The Russians deny to this day that they had Litinenko killed, in spite of substantial evidence that they were behind it. Israel denies any involvement in the 2010 killing of Mahmoud al-Mabhouh, in Dubai, and some of those assassins were on hotel videos. History is full of assassinations, and most of those are denied by the countries that pulled them off. There is a good reason for that. We are not dealing with rational leaders when we deal with terrorism. Terrorists don't have a home and they don't have to get re-elected. They blow up buildings and put an airplane into my wife's office in the Pentagon. Did I want to see Bin Laden dead after that? Of course, but there has to be plausible deniability. That is what covert means.

---

16 Graham Allison, *The Commission on America's National Interests*, John F. Kennedy School of Government, Harvard University, July 2000, page 7-10.

17 Edward Pound and David Rogers, *An Israeli Contract With a U.S. Company Leads to Espionage*, Wall Street Journal, January 17, 1992.

18 No Safe Haven, Iran's Global Assassination Campaign, Iran Human Rights Documentation Center, Appendix 1 "Chronological List of those Killed during the Islamic Republic of Iran's Global Assassination Campaign", May 2008, http://www.iranhrdc.org/english/publications/reports/3152-no-safe-haven-iran-s-global-assassination-campaign.html

19 Dr. Mathew Levitt, *Iranian Terror Operations on American Soil*, Testimony before a joint hearing of the House Homeland Security Subcommittee on Counterterrorism and Intelligence and Subcommittee on Oversight, Investigations, and Management, October 26, 2011

20 Joby Warrick, *Iran Bolsters Retaliation Capability in Persian Gulf*, Experts Say, Washington Post, 26 July 2012. http://www.washingtonpost.com/iran-bolsters-retaliation-capability-in-gulf-experts-say/2012/07/26/gJQAQuFUCX_story.html

21 Thom Shanker, Eric Schmitt & David E. Sanger, *U.S. Adds Forces to Persian Gulf, a Signal to Iran*, New York Times, July 3, 2012. http://www.nytimes.com/2012/07/03/world/middleeast/us-adds-forces-in-persian-gulf-a-signal-to-iran.html?_r=1&hp

22 Matthew Fisher, Harper Moves for Presence in Straight of Hormuz with Regina Deployment, National Post, http://news.nationalpost.com/2012/07/03/strait-of-hormuz-canada/

23 David E. Sanger, *Obama Order Sped up Waves of Cyberattacks Against Iran*, New York Times, June1, 2012, http://www.nytimes.com/2012/06/01/world/middleeast/obama-ordered-wave-of-cyberattacks-against-iran.html?pagewanted=all

24 Nicolas Falliere, Liam O Murchu, and Eric Chien, *W32.Stuxnet Dossier*, February 2011 (this appears at version 1.4 and originated in 2010) http://www.symantec.com/content/en/us/enterprise/media/security_response/whitepapers/w32_stuxnet_dossier.pdf

25 Ibid, page 6

26 John Markoff and David E. Sanger, *In a Computer Worm, a Possible Biblical Clue*, New York times, September 29, 2010 http://www.nytimes.com/2010/09/30/world/middleeast/30worm.html?pagewanted=all

27 Kim Zetter, *Researchers Connect Flame to US-Israel Stuxnet Attack*, Wired, June 11, 2012. http://www.wired.com/threatlevel/2012/06/flame-tied-to-stuxnet/

28 Siobhan Gorman, *Iran Renews Internet Attacks on U.S. Banks*, Wall Street Journal, 17 October 2012, accessed 30 October 2012, http://online.wsj.com/article/SB100008 7239639044459270457806306320164 9282.html

29 Daily Mail on line, *WikiLeaks cable 'led Iran to hang kick-boxer it claims was Israeli spy who assassinated nuclear scientist'* 16 May 2012, http://www.dailymail.co.uk/news/article-2145218/WikiLeaks-cable-led-Iran-hang-kick-boxer-said-Israeli-spy-assassinated-nuclear-scientist.html

30 Reuters, *Iran Airs 'Confessions' in Killings of Nuclear Scientists*, 6 August 2012, http://news.nationalpost.com/2012/08/06/iran-airs-confessions-in-killings-of-nuclear-scientists/

31 Judicial Watch Website, accessed 30 October 2012, *Judicial Watch Obtains DOD and CIA Records Detailing Meetings with bin Laden Raid Filmmakers*, http://www.judicialwatch.org/press-room/press-releases/13421/

32 CNN, *Workers Exhuming Yasser Arafat's Body in Probe of Death*, 5 November 2012

33 TASS, *London Coroner's Court to probe into Berezovsky's involvement in Litvinenko death*, 3 Nov 2012

CHAPTER 3

·····················

Real Secrets

We live in a secret-filled world without even realizing it. If all secrets were like National Security Information, they would have big letters at the top and bottom of a page that said something like "Top Secret". I can still remember the tingle I got on my neck when I got to see the first one of those, but it was years before I found out there were some Really Big Secrets that made some of those Top Secret things seems less important. Top Secret is not an expression of value; it is an expression of impact to the U.S. if something is given to people who are not authorized to have it. It isn't a good expression of that, either, as you will see.

There are a few secrets that can stop a person, and hold them in suspension. I remember a picture of a building and it was taken from ground level. Since I knew where that building was, it seemed impossible that anyone could have taken it and gotten it out of there. I just blurted out "I wonder who took that picture?" and then shut up. The people in our meeting looked at me like they just noticed I was a leper. Nobody was going to say where that picture came from or how it ended up where we were looking at it. Just thinking for a few seconds, before asking the question, would have been enough to realize the name of the person who took it (the source) was as important as the picture itself. The nature of secrets is that the source, and the way things are collected, is usually as important as *what* was collected. Woodward and Bernstein understood that.

So, when we asked ourselves about the list the President keeps on the terrorists who are going to hit by a drone strike, we might ask "How do we know what terrorists should be on that list?" That is a Really Big secret and one the ACLU is going to try to find out. How we know who belongs there, may be more important than the list itself, the drones, or the killing of terrorists. The names of the sources, and the ways we go about collecting things, is called Sources and Methods and they are one of the largest classes of secrets governments and businesses have. Reporters know this better than anyone, but the ACLU must not be far behind.

All the more odd that a double-agent appears in our early morning papers and on TV. Not only was he a source of some Really Big Secrets, but he was *not our source*. The White House said a plot to blow up an airplane had been discovered some months before and it was never a threat to anyone in the U.S. [34] They knew about it and had it under control. This is actually not something I want to hear, since there is a credibility problem with any government agency that says it has something under control. I get this mental image of a guy holding out his hand with sand in it, and the sand is spilling out everywhere.

John Brennen, White House Counterterrorism Advisor, and now the Director of the CIA, said this was a non-metallic bomb, [which would presumably get through metal detectors] but they were not going to speculate about whether it would or could get through an airport security system. They would leave the speculation for anyone who read the story. This is certainly odd, since there doesn't seem to be many reasons why a person would want to build a bomb that was non-metallic, and you can probably list them on one finger. Brennen added that this was why we have Intelligence Agencies out there protecting us - they keep us informed about what our enemies are up to. [35] He said this with a straight face, but he had a point. We do have a lot of intelligence people trying to keep up with what is going on in the world, and they are supposed to let us know when a person gets into a terrorist organization and gets hold of a bomb. It doesn't follow that they then make that information public.

This particular bomb was built by Ibrahim Hassan al-Asiri, a bomb-maker who was well known in the Middle East. [36] A few months before we heard about him in the news, his brother tried to blow up Saudi Arabia's anti-terrorism chief, Mohammed bin Navef, in a suicide bombing and some of Asiri's handiwork showed up in cargo planes bound for the United States. I stopped buying printer cartridges for a little while until they figured out where all of those bombs were. How we knew it was his handiwork is anyone's guess, but the fact that we knew was a pretty important secret to somebody, the person who tipped us off about what Asiri was up to.

On the 9th of May, we found out a little more about this person when the Los Angeles Times writers Ken Dilanian and Brian Bennet filed a story about how we got the information from a person who was said to be a CIA double-agent [37]. This is a class of people we do not see in the news very often, and if I were one of these guys, it would be my choice to not be in the news. My uncle once got his picture on the front page of a local newspaper and when he saw it, he had reason to be concerned. The newspaper was in Vietnam and so was he. The story said he was building a port facility there. That kind of thing can get a person killed, and this was the same sensitivity.

To make matters worse, the story says the Saudi Intelligence Service was helping the CIA with an operation in Yemen. Officials said the U.S.-Saudi counter-terrorism operation helped us track Fahd Mohammed Ahmed Quso, who recently became operations manager of Al Qaeda in the Arabian Peninsula, the Yemen-based faction that intelligence officials say poses the greatest danger to the United States. On the Sunday after, a drone strike killed Quso, so his place in the news, after this, is limited.

They traced this guy to Asiri and decided to get one of the bombs he was making so they could have a look at it. Rep. Peter T. King (R-N.Y.), chairman of the House Committee on Homeland Security, confirmed that getting the bomb and the drone strike were part of the same operation. Rep. Michael McCaul (R-Texas), a member of the Homeland Security Committee added that "They don't usually build just one; they build multiple." These are certainly secrets to somebody, though apparently not these two in Congress.

Then, Dilanian and Bennet added one more note:

> "U.S. intelligence officials had planned to keep the bomb sting secret, a senior official said, but the Associated Press learned of the operation last week. The AP delayed posting the story at the request of the Obama administration, but then broke the news Monday."

That story may have been Adam Goldman, [with credited help from Kimberly Dozier and Eileen Sullivan] in the Denver Post. [38] The press often holds stories that can cause a risk to life so the person can be protected before the news is released. That report says the CIA stopped a terrorist from boarding a plane with a new kind of underwear bomb. This had the White House and Homeland Security scrambling to explain how they were so sure there were no plans for an attack on the U.S. during the time when they knew there were attacks being planned. It is reasonable to expect nobody wanted to tip these folks off that we knew anything about it. ABC News then reported that "somebody inside the terrorist cell" probably didn't want this bomb to be used and stopped it. [39]

Certainly, if this person were to be discovered, he might be named by al Qaeda, so they could put a reward on his head. If the story had never become public, that might have happened anyway, since the bomb makers were not the kind of guys who like being tricked like this. They were probably not very happy about the way this went down. They certainly knew who they might want to look for, without reading it in the newspapers.

Newspapers, Intelligence agencies, and politicians know the value of a good source. They are hard to find and hard to keep as sources, since as time goes on, it becomes more dangerous to be one. They want to flip in and out of doing this kind of work when the stress gets to them. So, reporters and intelligence officials have to look for new ones all the time and try to encourage the ones they have to continue working. Being a source is a very stressful job, and there are a lot of people doing it who aren't very good at it.

The Reliability of Sources

Several years ago, I was at a government meeting with some secret kind of things going on when someone asked a really important question about our source: "How much of this are you sure about?" We had not even thought about it until he asked. The question is valid for any of these press reports, and for most of what anyone sees on the Internet.

All press people have their sources. They don't always just make up these things, or tap into phone message systems to find out what is going on. The Chinese have introduced a wrinkle to the business of having sources provide information to those outside their control, by going after the sources themselves. We should reasonably expect them to do that through their own internal network monitoring, which is extensive, but they have decided that wasn't working very well. They started hacking Bloomberg News, the New York Times and Wall Street Journal to find out where those sources in China might be located.[40] They were specific in what they were looking for, the sources of stories about the wealth of the Chinese leadership, but stole passwords for every Times employee and entered 53 accounts to look for the information they wanted. They probably know who the sources are now.

But, sources are sometimes people who are on the fringes of the things they are reporting on. They don't know much, but they know more than the reporter. Give twenty people a briefing on something really secret and there will be that many versions of it when it is repeated. This goes to the reliability of a source. We used to have a statement in law enforcement, "a source that has provided reliable information in the past". It says nothing about the reliability of the current information, but says the source did report things we validated after the fact. The source provided accurate information, which we know from hindsight. The reliability of these kinds of sources, who might be criminals themselves, was always a worry. Sometimes they have deals with a prosecutor to limit the amount of time they will have to be in jail, in exchange for certain information. When that comes up in court, juries always raise their eyebrows. Terrorists are worse. We can never be sure about the accuracy, so we usually would try to verify the information some other way.

We can be fairly sure this person did get a bomb out of the country because the FBI says they have it. Now, we know where it is, and we know there was a real bomb that the FBI obtained from someone. Al Qaeda may have been penetrated by this source, whether he was pretending to be a bomber, or not. We will never know what the involvement of another country's Intelligence Service was, because almost nobody in world talks about what their Intelligence Services are doing, with the possible exception of the United States. We will never know for sure if he did, or didn't, get into their inner circle, because Al Qaeda will never admit it. It would make them look bad. None of this can ever be verified, but it got into print anyway.

If he had the bomb, he must have gotten it from someone, and managed to get it out to the FBI. That someone might have been working for al Qaeda, but there are quite a few bombs floating around in the Middle East, so it is not hard to get one. It could have come from anywhere.

Quso and Asiri are dead, both killed by drone strikes. There are plenty of people who knew how they died, and a few probably didn't miss that missile flashing across the sky. A couple of them were probably people who lived in the neighborhood where they got whacked, and knew who Quso and Asiri were. Finding one of them to talk to, might be as difficult as trying to find a witness to a murder committed in front of two gangs fighting in the street. I tried to do that once and found a lot of blind people who are easily distracted when a gun goes off. Three of them were tying their shoes.

The rest of it is combination of things that might be true, might be misunderstandings of the truth, or might be speculation by "experts". Different country reporters may see the case in the slant of their own politics. The only people who know what is true, and what is not, are not going to say. Those people are generally ones who know how to keep quiet about something that will get one of their sources killed.

With every story like this, there is a lot of speculation being stated as fact. Usually, that is a good thing. If the operation was run by the U.S. government; if it was a covert operation; if it was successful in getting a bomb out of an Al Qaeda bomb factory, those are all the kinds of secrets that we are supposed to be keeping. All the more reason for people in government to keep their mouths shut about this kind of thing.

Diane Feinstein, who as the Senior Democrat on the Senate Intelligence Committee, probably does know what happened, said we should not blame the reporters. But, she added "This has to stop. When people say they don't want to work with the United States, because they can't trust us to keep a secret, that's serious."

Whether we blame reporters is something we have to decide for ourselves, using the Watergate measuring stick. For every person who says they can't work with us anymore, there are several who say, "I think I will just cut back my exchanges with you. It is getting a little hot out there." The ultimate effect is the loss of good people who want to remain anonymous.

But while we were still thinking about the source of the bomb, Diane Feinstein is more than halfway through New York Times reporter David E. Sanger's book "Confront and Conceal: Obama's Secret Wars and Surprising Use of American Power." ..., "You learn more from the book than I did as chairman of the intelligence committee, and that's very disturbing to me.'[41] Sanger had a good many sources to keep these stories all going at the same time. I admire him for the skill he has.

Debra Saunders, a freelance writer, says "the beltway has become a giant sieve", as if this was something new. The beltway she is referring to is the one around Washington D.C. and it has been a sieve longer than there has been a beltway. There just isn't anything anyone is doing about it. Some reporters seem to think this is a government problem, but it isn't unique in government. It is a whole earth problem.

Crime that Pays

We have many more secrets than we will ever admit, and not all of them are written down somewhere. Some are hidden away by personal choice; some are controlled by governments; some are business secrets that are part of our jobs. We have too many, of too many types, and we keep them too long - some, for all the wrong reasons.

There are companies like Enron, and the empire that made up Bernard L. Madoff Investment Securities, that have secrets. The fact that they exist for so long, and become so big, is testimony to their ability to keep them. This just shows that secret keeping has a bad side too, but "bad" is a relative term in cases like this. There are a few people who think Nixon was a good President and should have stayed in office. They thought Watergate was bad for the country.

Both Enron and Bernie Madoff had business reputations that were good in their field. Madoff, in 1990, was the Chairman of NASDAQ and had a solid reputation as a stock trader. Enron, the seventh largest company in the U.S. was not making money out of thin air. It operated for 15 years, had 21,000 employees in 40 different countries. It owned pipelines, energy sales operations and the largest power project in India.[42]

Authur Andersen was Enron's auditing company and they too had a good business reputation. The auditing business is one where secrets are a must and they had a few about how Enron had been doing business. Two days before Enron announced a $618 million loss, one of Authur Andersen's lawyers issued directions to people inside who had audited Enron, to destroy all but the most basic "work records" related to their audits. They were even authorized to work overtime to complete the task. This resulted in a criminal indictment of Andersen.[43,44] Andersen had a former employee, Sherron Watkins, who had gone to work for Enron and had identified some of the "special purpose entities" that allowed Enron to hide the financial situation the company was in. Enron told Andersen about an SEC investigation that was looking into these companies. The indictment says, two days later, they started a "wholesale destruction of documents at Andersen's offices Houston, Texas" that led to obstruction of justice charges against them.

Madoff had a few tricks for making sure his secrets were kept. For example, he had a special area on the 17th floor where only about 20 of his employees worked. [45] It took a special pass to get into this section of the company, and it was very well controlled. He had an old IBM computer in that room that everyone wondered why it was still being used. Limiting physical access and having control of the information were prudent things for a person running a company like this. He was careful to keep his secrets, even if we are skeptical about his reasons for doing it.

Most business trade secrets work the same way. They are only trade secrets as long as they are secret. When they become known to the world, they lose whatever advantage they gave the company that had them. They are different than patents, which are secrets for a limited time. Trade secret protection continues indefinitely until public disclosure of the secret, so if I tell my friend, who publishes an investor advisory, that we are going to buy one of our bigger competitors, that is giving up a trade secret. We have spent money to protect that secret for many months, but it is lost now.

Businesses have always have trouble keeping secrets when there is lots of interest in what they do. Apple issued subpoenas to several blogs and websites to disclose the sources of articles written about some of the products, including the new Tiger OS, they had coming out in 2004-2005. The suit claimed they were disclosing trade secrets and Apple had a right to ask for the sources, to protect themselves.

Patent law requires public disclosure of the means to reproduce an invention in exchange for a limited monopoly over the invention. An inventor must choose between either patent or trade secret protection; both cannot protect the same invention simultaneously.[46] In this case, Apple had chosen to use the latter.

Almost every year after that, Apple sent notices to several outlets trying to prevent the publication of some of this "advance" information about products they were going to release. There is more speculation on what Apple will release at these shows, than any other subject in the universe and it is all good publicity for them. The Electronic Frontier Foundation filed a petition on behalf of the reporters involved, citing in part, that they should not have to disclose their sources for this information. The court found in the journalists' favor.

So, Apple is in a quandary here. They have to protect their trade secrets, and some of them must be leaked to journalists. In the 2004 case, the court said Apple should have done an internal investigation first to see where the leaks were coming from. By 2007, when this case was decided, they must have finished that up. What the court was telling them is the same as courts have found in National Security cases, giving information to journalists is certainly a problem for them, but don't blame the journalists for what they publish. Figure out where the leaks are coming from, and stop them. This is really all the White House should be doing, but there are elections in 2014, and they are reluctant to blame someone in the White House for something that might cost them a lot of votes. In 2015, they might.

I'm somewhat sympathetic to Apple in this, because they are not offering up a candidate for public office. They can try as they might to deal with the thousands of parts and accessory vendors that make up their supply chain, and there is a limit to how much they can do. Yet, in order to do business, they need all of those suppliers. They can't stop the leaks. The Defense Department, with WIKILEAKS, the White House and Apple, are, seemingly, in the same boat.

34 BBC News, *Al Qaeda Yemen Plane Bomb Plot Foiled by 'Insider'*, 08 May 2012, http://www.bbc.co.uk/news/world-us-canada-17994493

35 Ewen MacAsKill, *Al Qaida (sic) Bomb Plot Thwarted by CIA*, The Guardian, 7 May 2012, http://www.guardian.co.uk/world/2012/may/08/al-qaida-airline-bomb-plot

36 Brian Ross, Richard Esposito, and Rhonda Schwartz, *Officials: More Al Qaeda Bombs Unaccounted for*, ABC Nightline, 7 May 2012 http://abcnews.go.com/Blotter/officials-al-qaeda-bombs-unaccounted/story?id=16297199#.T92akCtYvhM

37 Ken Dilanian and Brian Bennett, *Al Qaeda Bomb Plot was Foiled by Double Agent*, Los Angeles Times, 9 May 2012, http://articles.latimes.com/2012/may/09/world/la-fg-bomb-plot-20120509

38 Adam Goldman, *U.S.: CIA thwarts new al-Qaida underwear bomb plot*, Denver Post, posted 05/07/2012, http://www.denverpost.com/breakingnews/ci_20567362/u-s-cia-thwarts-new-al-qaida-underwear

39 Ibid, Brian Ross, Richard Esposito and Rhonda Schwartz

40 Nicole Perlroth, Hackers in China Attacked the Times in the Last 4 Months, New York Times, 30 January, 2013, http://www.nytimes.com/2013/01/31/technology/chinese-hackers-infiltrate-new-york-times-computers.html?pagewanted=all&_r=0

41 Debra Saunders, *Feinstein Takes On White House Leaks*, Real Clear Politics, 14 June 2012 http://www.realclearpolitics.com/articles/2012/06/14/feinstein_takes_on_culture_of_leaks_114480.html

42 BBC News, *Enron at-a-glance*, 22August 2002, http://news.bbc.co.uk/2/hi/business/1780075.stm

43 Daniel Kadiec, *Enron: Who's Accountable?* Time Magazine, 13 January 2002, http://www.time.com/time/magazine/article/0,9171,1001636,00.html

44 Indictment, U.S. District Court, Southern District of Texas, 03/07/2002, http://www.justice.gov/archive/dag/cftf/chargingdocs/andersenllpindictment.pdf

45 James Bandler and Nicholas Varchaver, How Bernie Did It, CNN Money, April 30, 2009, http://money.cnn.com/2009/04/24/news/newsmakers/madoff.fortune/

46 Uniform Trade Secrets Act, Legal Information Institute, Cornell University, http://www.law.cornell.edu/wex/trade_secret

CHAPTER 4

Too Many Secrets

National Security secrets belong to governments, but we sometimes forget that they are not just *our* government's. Every country has a few. If they share them with us, the fact they are sharing, itself becomes a secret. This can all get really complicated and was one of the side issues with WIKILEAKS release of the State Department memos. They clearly show we were saying different things to different countries, which may not make sense to some, but makes perfect sense in the world of secrets.

Let me break this down, since it seems confusing. If Israel wants to tell us some secrets about Iran, the fact that they give us that secret is National Security Information and marked with a classification. Israel is the source, so it is protected for that reason. The secret itself is also classified by Israel so they have marked it to reflect that. We remark it in English so everybody understands where it is on the hierarchy of secrets. We now have two secrets from the first one: (1) Israel is sharing secrets with the U.S. on Iran and (2) the cooling tower in that enrichment plant is really a boiler that is not cooling anything. It heats things up. We should have known that, we say, and we smile.

Now, we want to "reciprocate" with Israel, so we tell them a few things we know about the trucks that have been putting oil in the boiler and the people we notice hanging around the place. These are all secrets and the fact that we gave them to Israel is also a secret. Though this does get complicated, if we only deal with one country, we can follow along pretty well. We can just put all the secrets we have in the Israel bin.

But, we don't deal with just one country. Now Saudi Arabia and Egypt say they have a secrets about Iran that they want to share with us. They don't share too many things with Israel, so they would not want Israel to know that they were sharing this thing with us, and we would not want Israel to know that we had it. This becomes a secret that Israel is not allowed to see unless Saudi Arabia say it is OK to say where it came from. Good luck with that part. This may be confusing but it is international politics and a lot more complicated than Obama and Romney going at it.

It gets worse when we start sharing secrets with some people we normally wouldn't share anything with. Let's say the Russians have decided to tell us some things about Iran that they know and we don't. It happens. The Russians might know that the boiler is just part of the kitchen and not part of the reactor that we thought was being heated. They think it might help their friends in Syria, if we understood what the boiler was for. We can't tell anyone where this information came from because Iran and Russia are friends and Iran would not like it very much. We have to keep this secret from everyone else, so we don't tell the Israelis that we know it. This is where friendship is a matter of convenience, not love and affection.

What we don't know is that the French have already told Israel about this and a whole lot more. The Russians know the French gave this to Israel, but it is a secret they want to keep to themselves, so they don't tell us. Multiply this by the number of countries that are involved and you see what a complicated mess sharing secrets really is. It is almost easier to just hang onto them and not tell anyone.

In some situations, whether information can be shared goes to a review board made up of all the different agencies that are involved. This can be a simple thing like a briefing being given to a foreign government, or it can be a military exercise with thousands of participants from several different countries. I used to get to vote on this board and there were always some interesting things that we had to share. Each person represents an agency and gets a vote, almost like a democracy. One day, my boss told me to vote "no" on a certain type of information we were going to give to a country in the Middle East. It seemed pretty straightforward, since it was not the kind of information we had shared with other allies in the region, so there was no reason to share it with this particular country. So, I voted No, and there was not even a ripple in the fabric of the force over this. However, within the hour my boss's boss who was a 3-star General got calls from two 4-star Generals who really, really, really wanted to give this information to the other countries. He was busy testifying on the Hill on some budget hearing so he had us all gather in his office and wait. When our 3-star got back, he went over the issues and was pretty sure the vote was the right one. But, this is where the democratic principles slowly fade into the sunset. He agreed with our logic but gave us an interesting view of the discussions of the day: "Four stars beats three", he said.

I would have to write another book to cover the International Traffic in Arms regulations that have grown up over the years, but suffice it to say, these are ways of protecting secrets from export to some other countries and it is more confusing than any of the other secret things, if that is possible.... The Arms Export Control Act started all of this, and says that the President will designate a list of things that are defense articles and services. These are not necessarily classified, but can be, and include things like firearms, ammunition, launch vehicles for missiles, the missiles, rockets, torpedoes, explosives, "vessels of war"(ships that are used for sea battle), military electronics, guidance equipment, toxicological agents and radiological equipment. These are the kinds of things you would normally think of as war-making tools, so those things make sense. But, there are some other categories like "defense services not otherwise enumerated" and "miscellaneous articles" that lead to difficulties of interpretation. This is why votes are taken and nobody can be held personally responsible for making a mistake.

Other countries, particularly the Chinese, know about Export controls, licensing, trade secrets and all the rest of it, and they know how to get around our rules. They open a facility where they can develop research and they get different companies to guide them in that research. It doesn't look like export of technology, but it is. I got a valuable lesson in this from a professor at the University of Wisconsin, where I went to undergraduate school.

In the 80's I was assigned to an Industrial Security office, in Chicago, belonging to the Defense Department. Our job was to make sure people with government contracts were protecting the information the government gave to them, and part of that was following the export laws. I went out to these places and looked at what they were doing and how they were doing it, to see if the information was safe. Among other things, I looked at students attending colleges and whether or not some of the professors who work on government contracts were teaching foreign students things they were not supposed to export without a license. I'm not sure this kind of thing is still being done, but it was then. There is no such thing as academic freedom in the world of secrets, and the professors knew exactly what I was talking about.

I went to one professor and outlined my concern with his Chinese students taking courses in advanced computing networks, many of them being pioneered in the new ARPANET which was the beginning of the first Internet. It didn't seem to be possible to teach advanced computing and not get into some of the areas that were defined as export restricted. He listened while I went through this whole argument and he said, "OK, I'll tell you what I will do. I will let you come to class with me. It starts in an hour and there are two Chinese students, from the mainland, in the back of that class. You stop me if I get into anything that seems like it would be export restricted." It seemed more than fair, but I only had an hour to do research on export controls for advanced computer concepts. I had to call back to the office to get some help. By the time class started, I had some points of reference.

As the class went on, I started to see why the clarity of a licensing export license was preferable to a decision made on the spot. The concept of export controls was a lot harder when they were being applied to something that was part of a working arrangement like a class where people were asking questions and more than one person was answering them. There were articles from magazines, textbooks, and discussions all packed full of things that could have fallen into one of the concepts that was not supposed to be exported. These already appeared in the public press. So, did we have things that were already public showing up in the Export laws as something that could not be exported? Of course. Could we define what it was that we weren't supposed to export? Not very well. This is why the Chinese have decided to have shared research facilities and locate them in China. It is much harder for us to define "export" when we have combined operations working together on definable projects. Nobody ever said the Chinese were stupid, or that they ever missed an opportunity to steal from us.

Most of the things we protect are probably not secrets to begin with.

Smoke

Ninety percent of the things the government has that it says are classified, are probably over-classified or improperly marked, and a goodly portion of business secrets are the same.

That is a big percentage for most people to swallow, so let me explain the concepts that allow it to be true. It is mostly the fault of policies that govern how information is protected in computers, because that is where information is.

In government, when national security information enters a computer, either at a government office or a contractor working for the government, it is protected at the level the computer processes and not at the level of its creation. The holder of it has to do this until it is reviewed by a human being, hopefully, one who knows why it was made into a secret. This is not an easy thing to understand, but it is simple.

The Federal agencies have never figured out how to separate different levels of classified material in a computer, unless all the users have the same clearance level, like Top Secret. Most people, who don't work for the government, think it has this giant network of Top Secret, Secret and other types of things all mixed together and any government employee has access to the whole of it. The Feds pretend they can do this, but they don't, and they can't, which are really two separate things. It is not something they can dismiss saying they have procedures to do it that way, because they don't do it. It can be done, but it costs too much money to separate all those kinds of things in a computer, that most agencies won't fund it.

We have spent close to a billion dollars trying to figure out how this is going to be done, and have almost nothing to show for it. We gave most of that money to the National Security Agency to build things called Multi-Level Systems (MLS). If you say MLS to Congress, the members and staff will walk away and not look back, but the inability to do it has caused all secrets to be treated as if they were really more important than they are.

Since most computer systems can't do MLS, they duplicate the information across other networks. There are secret networks that process no higher than Secret National Security Information, and some that are Unclassified. If we move some Secret information over to a computer with Top Secret in it, the Secret gets protected as Top Secret while it is there. This makes for more information that is protected at a higher level than there really needs to be.

Regulated businesses have the same problem. They try to use Role Based access control and rights management programs to keep all the data separated, but the real problem with that is the number and type of secrets in the commercial world. They are required to keep track of thousands of pieces of information that have little intrinsic value to them, but a good deal to the people writing legislation in Washington.

Colin Zick, from Foley Hoag, published a list of 32 different types of information that might have to be protected for Privacy or Security-related reasons.[47] The more types of secrets we have, the harder it is to keep a secret, but we have quite a few:

Administrative Procedure Act. (5 U.S.C. 551, 554-558)

Cable Communications Policy Act (47 U.S.C. 551)

Cable TV Privacy Act of 1984 (47 U.S.C. 551)

Census Confidentiality Statute (13 U.S.C. 9)

The Children's Online Privacy Protection Act (15 U.S.C. 6501-6506)

Communications Assistance for Law Enforcement Act of 1994 (47 U.S.C. 1001-1010)

Computer Security Act (40 U.S.C. 1441)

Consumer Financial Protection Act of 2010 (Pub. L. No. 111-203, 124 Stat. 1376)

Criminal Justice Information Systems (42 U.S.C. 3789g)

Counterfeit Access Device and Computer Fraud Abuse Act of 1984 (18 U.S.C. 1030)

Driver's Privacy Protection Act of 1994 (18 U.S.C. § 2721)

Drug and Alcoholism Abuse Confidentiality Statutes (21 U.S.C. 1175; 42 § U.S.C. § 290dd-3)

Electronic Communications Privacy Act (18 U.S.C. 2510-21, 2701-11)

Electronic Funds Transfer Act (15 U.S.C. 1693, 1693m)

Employee Polygraph Protection Act (29 U.S.C. 2001, et seq.)

Employee Retirement Income Security Act (29 U.S.C. 1025)

Equal Credit Opportunity Act (15 U.S.C. 1691, et. seq.)

Equal Employment Opportunity Act (42 U.S.C. 2000e, et seq.)

Fair Credit Billing Act (15 U.S.C. 1666)

Fair and Accurate Credit Transactions Act of 2003

Fair Credit Reporting Act (15 U.S.C. 1681-1681(u))

Genetic Information Nondiscrimination Act (P.L. 110-233, 122 Stat. 881)

Gramm-Leach-Bliley Act (15 U.S.C. 6801-6809)

Health Insurance Portability and Accountability Act (42 U.S.C. 1306)

HITECH Act (Title XIII of Division A and Title IV of Division B of the American Recovery and Reinvestment Act of 2009, Pub. L. No. 111-5)

Privacy Act of 1974 (5 U.S.C. 552a)

Right to Financial Privacy Act (12 U.S.C. 3402)

Telecommunications Act of 1996 (47 U.S.C. 222)

Telephone Consumer Protection Act of 1991 (47 U.S.C. 227)

U.S.A. Patriot Act (Pub. L. 107-56)

Video Privacy Protection Act of 1998 (18 U.S.C. 2710)

For each one of these laws, and this is not all of them, there are protected classes of information, and usually more than one.

If the business is a bank, there is another set of these laws that apply.

If it is a Pharmaceutical business, there is another set.

There are probably some for agriculture, microbiology, cooking, and any number of other things. I will admit to never having heard of some of this legislation, but worked with the Patriot Act every day for a few years, while we chased terrorists. Still, most of these laws never do very much to motivate people to take action because it takes time for a bill to be passed, the rule setters to get organized and rules to be published. That will come. Trying to find terrorists was motivational, but occasionally overshadowed by some of the administration.

I looked up some of the laws, just to see what they are talking about, since the titles are not very helpful. It was easy to start with some of the ones I had not heard of before. The Video Privacy Protection Act says a company that rents video tapes "or similar audio visual materials" may not knowingly disclose to any person, *personally identifiable information* concerning any consumer's records, except under certain situations specified in the law. This type of law illustrates what we face with describing only what can be done, and not what can't. I would like to know that rental agencies, department stores, service departments, libraries, even my own company, could not give out that personally identifiable information whether it involves video rentals or not. Take for example, the Electronic Funds Transfer Act, which says almost the same thing about electronic bank transfers from automated teller machines.

There is law after law that does the same for various types of transactions, when we need one good one for all of them. I could even say we cannot allow the transfer of personal information unless it meets certain conditions. The length of this list only serves to emphasize the out-of-control process that allows the Congress and Federal Agencies to create new categories of information that require some protection. They forget that each of these has an effect on the people who have to do the work. Secrets get layered on top of one another without any sense to the process that produces them.

Probably the most difficult to follow is the set of laws that center around law enforcement and the Justice Department. I want to use one of their categories because these are secrets that are not National Security Information and not business secrets. The folks at Justice are in a world of their own when it comes to creating ways to keep secrets. To try to straighten it out, Justice has come up with a way of exchanging information called the National Information Exchange Model (NIEM), a bureaucratic ponzi scheme, that keeps state and Federal computer people busy with work that nobody in their right mind would want to do. Justice makes rules about law enforcement related things - stacks and stacks of rules - that have accumulated over hundreds of years, and NIEM is only one of them.

Second, information is contextual, and computers hold a good deal of that context. In my career, I helped to prosecute two espionage cases where the proof that something is classified is essential to the prosecution. We had to sift through quite a few documents before the attorneys could find ones that would hold up in court. Some things, when separated from the context of the case, were not classified to anyone. The informant said, "The moon was full on the 17th of November, so we had an easy time getting through the park and onto the train." OK, but there is nothing classified about this except the informant's name and that is not mentioned here. Ninety-nine percent of the things in the case might be unclassified, but someone will argue that anyone reading it would know who the source was, so they classify all of it. This is the idea that compilation of material produces something that is more important than all the parts, by themselves.

There is some truth in their concern, since there may have only been one train on the 17th of November and only five passengers got on it. We would have to look that up to find out. They might be able to figure out who the source actually was. But, I'm not going to court, trying to prove any of it is National Security-related unless it is clear that the information was classified for a valid reason. Being sure about what somebody can figure out is not easy for anyone. The prosecutors will just keep looking. Eventually, the attorneys find something that looks, and really is, important enough to be classified. In a later chapter, I focus on some of the difficulties of making and keeping something classified for National Security reasons.

Mirrors

The third thing is bigger than anything Washington can make. The value proposition for secrets is not very sound. There are formal things that everyone recognizes as something that needs to be protected, like the formula for Coca-Cola, with a singular value that is measureable. The value of a Really Big Secret is not so easy to esti-mate. How much do we lose if leaders of the world discover that astral projection is not just a science fiction writer's dream? As long as we can do it and nobody else knows about it, what we can discover this way is really valuable. When the rest of the world knows about it, they start trying to figure out what to do about it. They are going to try to keep those people from Board or Cabinet Meetings and figure out how to do it for themselves. Once everyone can do it, the value of it will be less. Coca-Cola understands that better than anyone.

There are also too many secrets that have a value that is hard to measure. How much is the information that makes up my identity worth? Businesses break up the pieces so I never know where they are, and governments make them public for many different reasons that I wouldn't agree with. It is something I can't control, but the con-sequences of their actions fall on me. It would be different if I were doing something wrong. If I am part of a breakfast club that talks about what price we will put on butter we sell next week, the fact that we discuss this subject is a secret. It is also potentially illegal.

I can say I attend breakfast every Friday morning with my friends, and even put it on my schedule at the office. The value of this secret, in dollar terms, is the money we get that is greater than the amount that we would get if we didn't talk about the price at all. That part is never written down. Maybe too, we might add the value of time in jail, if we get caught. This is harder to figure out, but some prosecutor will be looking for the value of it if this ever gets discovered. He is not going to jury and say, "They conspired to fix prices but didn't make any money at it." It may be criminal to fix prices, but you have to make money or nobody is going to be interested in prosecuting. That is the way politics works.

At times, secrets serve a purpose. It allows regulators to simul-taneously close down banks in eighteen countries and put restrictions on forty-four others when they were identified as having been guilty of 'fraudulent conduct on a worldwide scale'. The indictment of eight bank employees, in 1988, for laundering money for the Medellin drug cartel was the first anyone heard of the Bank of Credit and Commerce International (BCCI). BCCI was the CIA's bank for maintenance of secret accounts that were financed Afghan rebels and bribed General Noriega of Panama.[48] If I were guessing, I would say that somebody in CIA is still protecting the fact that they used BCCI to finance anyone in Afghanistan. I can almost guarantee that NSA is still protecting the fact that they monitored the cell phone of Umar Farouk Abdulmutallab, even though the White House said they were doing it. What this does is put us in the position of protecting some really important secrets that anyone could know, if they look. I don't think we can afford to do that anymore.

My cousin's problem with drugs fall into the same category. It might do harm to his family if it got out, but we really can't say what the value of that secret might be. It is really hard to put a value on my cousin's reputation, and only slightly easier to put a value on that Coke formula. But, if you asked 100 people which of those secrets is more important, I would bet that 99 of them would say the Coke formula, because this is a secret they can understand as being of great value.

So, the problem with secrets is that we don't have a good way to measure the value of them. Businesses tend to think of things in terms of a dollar figure, so they measure risk of some secret in terms of its value to them and the cost to protect that value. The formula for this is Risk= Probability of Occurrence times the Impact. I have heard this called the sum of two guesses, both of which are wrong. Nobody can accurately measure the chance that something might happen, so they guess. Yes, I know there are tables of actuaries that can predict about when a person will die, but it does me little good to know that the average person lives

20 years longer than I have. They have lots of data for things like that, but I don't want to die to prove them right or wrong. Neither does the woman who was killed when a tree fell into her bedroom during a storm we had last week. But they don't have as much data about the water pipe freezing in a cold winter and dumping the sewage into our new data center.

Nobody can accurately measure the impact on the company, so they guess. The sewage was cleaned up and we lost some equipment and some data, but only a day's worth… or so. "Or so" usually means we don't know for sure how much data we lost, but we think not much, because "lots" is not the right answer for the guy I work for, or the shareholders. The chances of anyone finding out what we talk about at the Friday breakfast is harder to compute, and we can only talk about that among ourselves. We certainly can't bring in any of those Risk Analysis professionals we have working for us. We may not even think about that risk, or dismiss it as "not likely".

The sum of those two guesses is always wrong, but we can find a few vendors who will automate the process and produce a result with nice graphs. It just makes guessing more colorful without giving accurate results of the loss. But if we can measure the value of that loss in billions of dollars, the importance of them is measureable by a standard any manager can recognize. That doesn't mean they act on it. Human beings always think they are better than the idiot from the other company, or "we can accept the risk."

The government uses a measure of the damage the disclosure of its secrets will cause to the United States, and that is even harder to measure than the Risk. If the White House says NSA is monitoring cell phone calls of potential terrorists overseas, they are saying release to the public of that fact is not going to cause any harm to the United States. If NSA says that same fact is Top

Secret, they are saying the loss of that secret will cause extremely grave damage to the United States. One of them is wrong, but we don't have a real good way of figuring out which one. The White House spends very little protecting a fact that NSA spends millions of dollars a year to keep secret. There is no logic in this, and there are big debates around on the White House, Congress and NSA sides of this, producing only opinions and no action.

The fourth problem with secrets is we can't keep the ones we have. They leak all over the place and we can't seem to do very much about it. This is the problem of trying to protect everything; we end up doing badly at protecting much of anything. Secrets leak because there are far too many of them and no good way to say which ones are really the ones that are most important. The other aspect is the lack of any deterrent to leaking.

Fifth, technology has a lot to do with why secrets are no longer very safe. There are two sides to this. First, we have given every person an opportunity to give up secrets by handing them smart phones and computers. Because they can do it, they do. We have pushed the technology down to the individual and not all individuals even look at policies before they act. Imagine that, if you will. They have the power to decide for themselves what is an important secret and what isn't. Sometimes they are not very good at it.

It is also true that computers are not safe places to put secrets, yet that is where they are. The movement to cloud and big data technologies takes some of the laws government monitoring and audit of leaks out of the hands of the owner of the data. We let users bring their own data devices to work and use them and we are auditing and monitoring someone else's device. That will get to court one day.

We should think a little bit about not putting so many Really Big Secrets in computers that are connected to each other. I could guess that the Coca-Cola formula is not on a computer with any kind of connection to the Internet. There used to be a rule in government computer systems that no Top Secret computer could be connected to a computer that was Secret and connected to the Internet. That gave a person on the Internet a chance to get into a Top Secret system. It was very hard to do, but it was a path in. We got rid of that rule long before the Internet became the Wild West.

Judging from the number and types of secrets that are tossed around in the newspapers and on blogs, that may be resulting in more leaks of secrets than anyone really wants. It is dangerous and it will get worse. We never really know if people are doing it on purpose, or made an innocent mistake. They talk too much, and they are not very careful about what they talk about. It doesn't much matter what the motivation is, political tiffs, a better gaming experience, teen-age power struggles, business competition, or government cover-ups, the heat of the moment, and the technology, can do immeasurable harm. We are telling our enemies things we have never told them before, and shouldn't be telling them now.

---

47 Colin J. Zick, "Security and Privacy in 2011: How to stay a step ahead," (Jan. 2011), slide 2, PowerPoint presentation available at http://www.securityprivacyandthelaw. com/2011/01/articles/recent-legislation-1/security-and-privacy-issues-of-2011-how-to-stay-a-step-ahead-of-the-coming-wave-of-legislation-and-selfregulation/ Used with permission, but no longer posted.

48 James Adams and Douglas Frantz, *A Full Service Bank*, Pocket Books (New York, New York) April 1992, page 5-6.

CHAPTER 5

....

Other Peoples' Secrets

One of the best stories about the keeping of secrets is the Kurt Eichenwald's book *The Informant*[49]. It is a story of price-fixing involving several companies; the main story centers around Archer Daniels Midland Company which, he says, established bogus industry associations to cover the activities that were needed to get together on matters of sale of some of their products. The informant is Mark Whitacre, a real person with a PhD, who was President of the Bioproducts Division of ADM.[50] The book opens with the FBI visiting some of the senior managers of ADM and laying out a small piece of what they knew. After that, it was not hard for the ADM folks to figure out that there was someone on the inside telling the FBI what was going on. You could imagine the anxiety of a person who knows they know, just as Felt knew the White House knew, and having to go to work every day, just like the day before. It is a little like being a spy. Going to meetings creates anxiety about the folks around who might be taking notes for law enforcement to read. They might be recording things. In the end, Whitacre was treated like a criminal and sent to jail, so the life of an informant does not guarantee the person protection from any criminal act they may have committed. That kind of protection goes to people in witness protection, who commit crimes much worse than what he did. This somehow doesn't seem fair, but is the justice of Washington politics.

Eichenwald paints a grim picture of ADM and their previous run-ins with government investigations of one form or another and he says they had "…thanks to their scorched-earth tactics, the company had always won.[51]" This is what lawyers are paid for and we shouldn't be critical of them for looking out for their clients' interests. It goes with their oath. They protect both the guilty and innocent the same way, which is also the nature of secret keeping. They identify the secrets that have to be kept and they make sure they are kept from the other side. There is a practical reason for this, and we accept it. In big companies, somebody is always getting sued.

There is a nice little case going on with GlaxoSmithKline, which has apparently agreed to settle a suit against them brought by the Justice Department. They were supposed to be "offering incentives" to doctors to write prescriptions for certain drugs they made, the same thing the Chinese are accusing them of. The settlement in the U.S. is near $3 Billion, which seems to be a lot of money for this type of behavior. The Wall Street Journal report of this says,

> "The government's case against Glaxo was based partly on a lawsuit filed by former Glaxo employees in federal court in Boston in 2003. Thomas Gerahty, a former senior marketing development manager, and Matthew Burke, a former regional vice president, filed a so-called *qui tam* suit against Glaxo on the government's behalf under the Federal False Claims Act, which prohibits people or businesses from defrauding the government, and provides incentives for those who suspect wrongdoing to come forward." [52]

Prosecutions for this type of thing happen hundreds of time a year, though usually not for an amount so large, or so widespread. There are cases of product liability, environmental concerns, some type of civil action against a manager of some sort, labor actions and a thousand other things. It is important to the bottom line to get this right. At ADM, it was a $25B failure that was a valuable lesson to other companies doing the same thing. We need to think about what the lesson might be.

"Do the right thing" seems to come easily to mind, but that isn't good thinking. It could just as easily be "Stonewalling is good". Even with inside information, both governments and businesses can make it difficult to find enough to criminally prosecute. Prosecutors know this, so they learn the game rules pretty fast. We have to think about the kind of business conduct that falls out when keeping these kinds of secrets is encouraged.

Raj Rajaratnam, the founder and head of Galleon and a portfolio manager in Galleon Technology companies, was indicted in December 2009. He wasn't the first person to get information he wasn't supposed to have and use it to make money, but he was the first to get 11 years in prison for doing it.[53] Nobody will ever know all the interconnections of people and companies that were at work in this case, because not everything that makes up a case ends up in court. We saw a good example of that when Jerry Sandusky, a Penn State football coach, got convicted of 48 counts of child abuse but had other people who were abused as children, including one of his own adopted children, who were willing to testify. In the same way, not all of the people in the Galleon case will ever be known. Their names will be secrets, some of them for reasons we will also never know. In the end, there were more than 50 people prosecuted, but not every guilty person.

Businesses are usually clever at protecting the things that make money for the shareholders – the amount of money they are going to make in the next quarter, companies they are going to buy, or how they are going to merge or reorganize a business area. These kinds of corporate secrets are among the best protected in the world, because company officers have a legal obligation to protect them.

What Rajaratnam was doing was sharing information, normally something everyone does with friends, and using that information to decide when to buy and sell securities of various types. I don't have any friends who deal in securities, so that part would be different for me. In order to do that, he needed to have people who had direct access on the Board of Directors. One of those people, Rajat Gupta, was on the Board of Directors of Goldman Sachs, convicted for his part in an investment banking firm that tells other people, and businesses, how to invest their money. He was also on the Board of Proctor and Gamble, which makes almost everything, including money.

Gupta is now appealing his conviction and almost every story about it uses the term "allegedly" when saying he did anything wrong. It doesn't take much thinking to figure out why. The concept of lawyers defending clients' business reputations is hardly new, but this aspect of it is. These have managed to keep his innocence a subject of debate, even after he was convicted in court. You have to admire this idea. We usually say, a person is innocent until proven guilty. So, when the jury says "guilty" we should be able to drop the *alleged* qualifier.

The indictment says, in 2003, Gupta and Rajaratnam were doing $2 million in business together in Galleon's offshore accounts. Who has offshore accounts has come up more than once, and we tend to think of Switzerland, when we think about them, but the Cayman Islands has made a business of this type of transaction. The Caymans and Switzerland seems to be able to keep the financial shenanigans of a lot of people a secret and other countries are finding out it is a good way to make money. But, they make money because they keep the names of companies, and humans in them, secret, not because they are necessarily involved in criminal activity.

This was the beginning of the deals that started to get bigger as the associations got more complicated. They set up a couple of other companies and started trading in other types of overseas operations. Some of these accounts had tens of millions of dollars of Gupta and Rajaratnam's money.

The Justice Department said that Gupta and Rajaratnam knew what they were doing. They traded secrets that benefited both of them and allowed them to make more money, but they were violating the laws of trading while they were doing it. Gupta was supplying the information from the Boards of Goldman and P&G. Rajaratnam was making the deals and keeping things going. I was surprised that some of the trade and business publications thought this was not a crime, but more the typical way friends operated in the community. Maybe it is more common than most of us want to admit, or maybe that is just the flaying of folks who would love to be involved and were left out.

One of the secrets turned out to be that Goldman was not going to make a profit for the first time and the calls he made to report this were wiretapped by the FBI. But, there was an interesting sidelight to this case that had very little to do with insider trading. The wiretaps given to the Galleon attorneys were claimed, by them, to be secrets that could not be shared with the other defendants. Some of those defendants were the ones on the other end of that taped conversation. Judge Rakoff sort of said, "nice try, but give up those recordings to the other defendants where there is a need." [54] The claims of secrecy are everywhere and this is just one example of how they are used to protect interests, whether justified or not. Sometimes, it is just as important to know when something that is claimed to be a secret, is not.

Throughout the indictments of Galleon, and several others who followed, were indications that others "persons known and unknown" by their description, were involved. Some of these people are indicted, but the indictments are sealed, meaning they are not presented in open court for everyone in the companies being investigated, to see. This makes sense to anyone trying to protect a secret thing like this, but they are never charged and Gupta was. Who we are wiretapping and why, are also sealed because as soon as someone finds out their friend is being wiretapped, nobody will call them anymore. Eventually everyone will know, but the excitement that leads up to finding who did it is worth the wait.

This is a tricky area for a prosecutor because some of those people are talking and some of them are not. Some may be suspects, and probably all of them are guilty of something if they were participating in schemes that used insider information to make money. There are masses of these kinds of people in criminal courts and they are hard to keep track of sometimes. Some of them will plead guilty and some have to be prosecuted. People who are helping the investigation may get credit for that in the way they are punished and in when they are prosecuted. Some people will go along for a while until they see how much evidence has been collected and then plead guilty. There are secrets on both sides of this type of thing, and generally speaking, the longer they are kept, the better for the person keeping them.

What some employees miss, in the prosecutorial smoke on both sides, is the decision to stonewall, or report the incident and try to mitigate the losses it may cause, is a management decision. It has to be made consciously, with a clear understanding of the risks it will create. In both government and business, the decisions that are made are most often made by someone too far down the chain to accept the risk. If the IRS decides to screen the tax exempt status of TEA Party groups more closely than other more liberal groups, the Washington press wants to know how high up this type of behavior was encouraged, sanctioned, or ordered. If the person who took the risk, deciding to go ahead with the policy, was in a Field Office in Cincinnati, we can say that person was accepting a risk for everybody above them in the IRS food chain. That person will be called a "rogue employee" when discovered. If the person was risk averse, he might check with a manager somewhere in Washington to see if the policy was acceptable. That moves the acceptance of risk up a level, to where it more rightly should be.

This is the reason I have always liked the idea of an Ombudsman, someone inside the organization who can listen to what someone sees as injustice, and decide whether it needs to go higher up in the decision chain. People who don't have an outlet will go the press or the shareholders and it may be something even the senior managers would not have agreed to, had they had a say in the beginning.

So the secrets of this kind of case involves those of the members of Boards of Directors, traders governed by the Securities and Exchange Commission, different countries where the trades were taking place, trade secrets and competitive information of different companies, attorneys and their clients, law enforcement investigations, prosecutors, judges, and persons known and unknown. This is a little sliver of secrets that we deal with every day.

---

49 Eichenwald, Kurt, The Informant, (Broadway Books, New York, New York) 2000.

50 Extracted from Mark Whitacres Website, 12November 2012 http://www.mark-whitacre.com/index2.html

51 Eichenwald, page 6

52 Jeannie Whalen, Devlin Barrett, Peter Loftus, Glaxco in $3 Billion Settlement, Wall Street Journal, 3 July 2012, http://online.wsj.com/article/SB100014240527023042997 04577502642401041730.html

53 Susan Pulliam and Chad Bray, Trader Draws Record Sentence, Wall Street Journal, 13 October 2011, http://online.wsj.com/article/SB1000142405297020391430457662 7191081876286.html

54 U.S. District Court, Southern District of New York, Securities and Exchange Commission vs. Galleon Management LP, et. al. 02 September 2010, http://www. scribd.com/doc/26631796/Judge-Rakoff-Order-in-Galleon-Case

CHAPTER 6

Secrets with Sex

Our world leaders are not the best examples to hold up to our children, at least when it comes to their sex lives. The relationships between men and women, or men and men, women and women, have long been entertainment for the poor and a fascinating diversion for other people with money. We absolutely love reading about it, watching it on TV and, where possible, thinking about the possibilities of where it might lead. It takes a good moral compass to stay out of the swamp on this one, and not very many of us have one. Some people who think they do, are just waiting for the right opportunity, or they have a good one, and love the punishment from the hand of God that comes from getting caught with a bad one. Hypocrites abound here.

We have had some examples in the last couple of years that make all the watchers of the moral compass check to see if it is still working anywhere, but let me start with a couple of them who were not supposed to be in the news.

We have Dominique Strauss-Kahn, the head of the International Monetary Fund, and "Mr. Clean", who has strayed from his path and taken up with an attractive woman writing a book for him. As it turns out, she is only one of the people writing that book and this is the part that fascinates me, as a writer. Her co-author is Vernon Loeb of the Washington Post, who apparently knows nothing of the relationship between the two of them and plans to write a little something for the Post about what he doesn't know.[55] It isn't ghost writing, but we have to wonder who was writing all those things about General David Howell Petraeus, since hardly anyone needs two co-authors.

More books will be written about General Petraeus than he would have ever wished to be done, and it will not completely go away until the "whole story" i.e. how long we can keep this story going and sell print, is willing to play out. Three years after Tiger Woods ran his car into a tree at the end of his driveway, women are still popping up and saying they had sex with him, and a couple of others at the same time. Some of them are gorgeous, and most men can forgive him a little for letting the moral compass steer past true north. The problem is we will never know the truth of any of it until Tiger decides to write a book, *The Truth According to Tiger,* and that will probably be written by somebody else. It is hard to find truth unless it is *according* to somebody. We forget that sometimes.

It is especially hard when we have U.S. politics, French politics, New York, Washington, the CIA and the FBI. This is just like Watergate, except there is nobody in the Washington Post who can write the kinds of stories that were written about President Nixon. Newspapers are not what they used to be, but in this case, it hardly matters. They both get plenty of ink on the screens of computers. These two have all the elements of a spy novel, except they are missing guns. Both cases are people who work in Washington, but that could just be a coincidence. Both become public when they should have been kept a secret.

The IMF is a beautiful, but stuffy place to visit, just off the main street leading up to the Hill and Congress, and a long walk to the White House, except in the summer. The CIA is not an easy walk to anywhere, and even though everyone knows where it is, now that they have street signs up telling everyone, it is not easy to see from the roads that surround it. You can't walk into either one of these places because they are both well guarded, but for different reasons.

People don't even think about the IMF very often, but that is the nature of their work. The IMF says it "promotes international monetary cooperation and exchange rate stability, facilitates the balanced growth of international trade, and provides resources to help members in balance of payments difficulties or to assist with poverty reduction". They sound like a civic group, and that is the kind of thing that puts people to sleep around here, with the possible exception of throwing arrows at China for currency manipulation. It is a long time between those kinds of events. So, nobody really knows very much about the IMF, and not very many people care either.

The CIA is different. Anybody who knows anything about the CIA, knows they don't know very much. They probably know more about the IMF. I'm not even sure, after working with them, off and on for 45 years, that I know anything at all about them. Nobody knows what their budget goes for or how much they get of the $80 billion in the Intelligence budget. I actually learned some things I didn't know from their new website.

Most of the stories I have heard from CIA people are funny. They don't like to say anything, but when they do, they like to tell someone what has happened to make their day a little brighter. Spying is not that kind of thing. It is stressful, boring, and on the fringes, dangerous. It isn't dangerous very often, unless they go to someplace where there are no funny stories, like Iraq, Afghanistan, or Libya. Most of the spying part is done by the National Clandestine Service, that "strengthens national security and foreign policy objectives through the clandestine collection of human intelligence (HUMINT) and Covert Action."[56] It never sounds like spying when someone says it like that.

What the CIA really does is analysis of "facts" so that our government officials can act on them. That part is done in the Office of Intelligence and Analysis, "where incomplete and sometimes contradictory information is transformed into unique insights that inform US policy decisions. Members of the DI help provide timely, accurate, and objective all-source intelligence analysis on the full range of national security and foreign policy issues to the President, Cabinet, and senior policymakers in the US government." That kind of statement makes me tingle all over, but I love these people who work behind the scenes and try to get something out that is accurate and not filled with a lot of opinions of people who just want to be quoted.

Spying is the collection of facts, from various sources, and putting it together so it is readable by a human being. Analysis is the really important part that happens after that. CIA can decide, based on thousands of facts of various types, that something is true, and will be true for X-amount of months, given the quality of the information they have. They usually don't mention the word "truth" in any of their analyses, because it is a moving target, and subject to political bending. But, people in Washington want the raw data so they can decide for themselves if something is true or not, and they want to take only the things that help support the position that they have already taken. They try, every now and again, to get the CIA to temper what they have said about something to fit their own facts, rather than the analysis, and I have seen this get pretty testy in some of the Congressional Committees. This is what makes living in Washington so interesting. There are no end to *facts* to make Washington sing, and they don't like it when CIA sings a different song. Every day, The Agency makes some enemies because of it. I saw it make a man very uncomfortable.

The General I worked for was constantly testifying before one Congressional Committee or another because our organization, Ballistic Missile Defense, had a lot of money. Agencies with money, and people with money, are generally not liked very much in Washington, though it is hard to understand why - maybe it's jealousy. One day, he had to testify about an analysis of the threat posed by North Korean long-range missiles to the United States. This was a hot political statement because the White House wanted the CIA to say that North Korean missiles couldn't hit the U.S. and they could then justify not putting very much money into missile defense. CIA thought a better telling of the truth was that the missiles couldn't hit the Continental United States, just the box defined by Maine, Florida, Arizona, and the state of Washington, but they could hit Hawaii and Alaska. Both sides of this were exposed in the Washington Post, but nothing was really said about the National Intelligence Estimate (NIE), which is what the CIA calls this kind of thing. It was Top Secret, so people would say they had read it, and pretend that their side was somehow expressed in the NIE. This is the advantage of some types of secrets. You can pretend to know them, even if you don't, and half of Washington will never know.

The General was asked some very pointed questions about whether there was enough money in his budget given the threat by North Korea, and these are hard to answer without looking like someone who wants more money and would say anything to get it. He was cool about it, sticking to the statements that were allowed to be made in an open session, i.e. that missiles could not hit the Continental United States. Some of the other people asking questions were not very clear about what part of the U.S. we were talking about, but that fit their intensions to cut the funding.

To try to clarify what was being discussed, Senator Inoye, from Hawaii, asked if the General knew Hawaii was in the United States. It was a softball question, but got the point across. The other Senators were not so happy about this line of questioning and started debating with the General about all the rest of his answers, to the point that he was accused of "siding with the Administration" on his responses. I felt sorry for him, but was also glad I wasn't testifying that day. The CIA tries to straddle a line that makes politics easier to do by both sides doing it.

So, when the leaders of the IMF and the CIA are both caught having affairs with another person, each one has a lot of practical experience dealing with the delicate nature of the politics involved. Mr. Strauss-Kahn, who is a citizen of France, and was assumed to be on a track towards its Presidency, is on his way to the airport in New York when he is arrested by the local police and charged with assaulting a woman who was cleaning his executive suite at the Sofitel Hotel, New York. This is not something that happens every day, even in New York, and must have been a difficult case to handle. New York police have the experience of the United Nations to guide them in such things, so they know quite a bit about international stars and their activities when they get away from home. But even in the annuals of interesting behavior, this one is more interesting than some. Initially, it looked like this bad man forced this working woman to have oral sex, then ran away hoping to get to another country before he could be arrested. He was said, by the French press, to have done these kinds of things before, and caused the populace there to have doubts about the toleration of this kind of behavior in their country. [57]

The fate of Mr. Petraeus is somewhat the same, but the facts-in-evidence are quiet a bit different. Through what has to be the most bizarre set of investigative circumstances ever to have come through the Justice Department, the Director of Central Intelligence is accused of having an affair with his biography writer and travelling companion, Paula Broadwell, who is the one being investigated.

Having an affair is usually not a crime by itself, depending on where a person lives. In Washington D.C., it is a capital crime and decapitation follows, unless of course, the person is "protected", or in French, *coverte*. The word actually comes from its use in the French Revolution to absolve people from the guillotine, which happened rarely. This concept may be new to some, and has nothing to do with the wearing of condoms or birth control, though there have been times when either one would have allowed a person who was not otherwise protected to appear to be so.

Protection is close to the use of the word *covert* as it is used today, i.e. there must be plausible deniability for the accused to have any chance of protection. John Edwards, former Senator from North Carolina, was in that class of people who have no protection because the covert nature of the offense was lost by a paternity test.[58] His deceased wife was tortured by the accusations of infidelity, but the rest of the world moved on. The Justice Department did not, and found it necessary to prosecute him for campaign violations based on accusations that his campaign manager, who had accepted responsibility for the baby, had misused funds given to him by Senator Edwards. He supported the baby of his videographer, Rielly Hunter, keeping them away from the press, something the Justice Department thought was misuse of campaign money. This was like sticking a sword in a dead man, but the trial came to nothing, a mistrial. Justice then decided it was OK to drop all the charges since the body was now full of holes and was not coming back to Washington where the beheading could take place. Another opportunity lost.

There seem to be some differences between France and the United States on how such matters are handled, and I'm not sure which of those would be correct. In my own house, my wife has said that having an affair was not a good thing and was not tolerated, whether against the law or not. The French do not seem to view it the same way. Anne Sterling, who had a career before marrying Strauss-Kahn, was well off and enjoying a good life by writing, which makes her a hero, automatically. She had been married for 20 years and, by all accounts is still married to the man. She stood by him in New York. She apparently kicked him out of the house, but not for his behavior there.

A year later, he was again under investigation by the French police for possible rape, and certain sex, with people who were prostitutes. Here again, this is not a crime in France, where almost anything related to sex is not a crime. There were a few of these sex parties with groups and he was accused of being involved with them, but denied knowing the women involved were prostitutes nor that there was violence used against any of the women. I have to admit, I like Sharon Waxman's characterization of this as the coming to life of *Eyes Wide-Shut*, [59] a movie I never understood, but watched twice, trying to understand what I was seeing. It's obvious the events were over the past few years. The key ingredient here seems to be the violence against women, not the affair, is the only criminal part of it. The political part is that Strauss-Kahn has been unable to find a suitable job and his party lost the election.[60] Now, he is kicked out.

The Director of Central Intelligence (DCI) was not having this kind of "affair" with Paula Broadwell, and, by comparison, nothing happened between them that couldn't be repeated in open court with children present. It would not have come to that anyway, because the Justice Department appeared to be willing to let the whole thing blow over by keeping it a secret. Remember, Justice does criminal investigations, so it would not be too difficult for them to say that it was not a criminal offense. They used this as justification for not telling anyone in the White House or the Intelligence Committees on the Hill, until after the election was over.

Plausible deniability is an essential part of the covert nature of secrets. Whether they told CIA was another question that was missing from the accounts. They certainly told them after-the-fact, but they should have told them when they knew. Diane Feinstein, Majority leader on the Senate Intelligence Committee, was not a happy person on CNN, when she said she did not like hearing about the DCI's resignation from the press. She was obviously missing one important ingredient. The election was only a month off, and this kind of publicity was a *distraction* to everyone. If we are totaling up plusses and minuses for Justice, let's give them a plus for that one. They can keep a secret when they want to.

However, the problem with moral compasses, is that some people have theirs calibrated differently than others. Among the other characters in this drama are Jill Kelley and her husband who are friends with the Petraeus family, and an FBI agent who is not the case agent for the Petraeus-Broadwell investigation, but is a friend of Jill's. He sends Jill a picture of himself, shirtless, "as a prank".[61] I think we all remember the "prank" defense from Representative Anthony Weiner who was sending e-mails of himself and claimed his Twitter account was hacked as a prank, sending out these pictures of men, not him. Then, as more information came out, more pictures, and some penetrating questions from ABC News and some independent bloggers, Weiner confesses to having sent the pictures and admits to "terrible mistakes" sending e-mails to six women over a couple of years. [62] Now he runs for Mayor of New York and all is forgiven.

Occasionally, journalists can get to something politically sensitive and make it public. But, people in the FBI apparently did more than just send Jill a picture. Just as a minor point of focus, the FBI works for the Justice Department.

In late October, House Majority Leader, Eric Cantor gets a call from an FBI employee notifying him that something was up with the investigation of Petraeus. Representative Dave Reichert arranges the call after he receives a call from another FBI official. Of course the FBI knows this, since in their interviews, both Petraeus and Broadwell admitted it, but they interview both again. A few days later, Cantor's Chief of Staff calls the FBI Chief of Staff to tell him about the call.[63] In the world of secrets, this is backdoor diplomacy. We are telling someone we know something that they think is a secret, but we know may not be as much of a secret as they think. If the matter blows up in their faces, they know someone will ask what they knew and when they knew it. This changes the politics of keeping a sex secret, making it harder to keep. It is a game of blackmail from that point on.

The essence of a sex secret is whether it could be used by someone else to blackmail the guilty parties. It has nothing to do with the morality of what they did. It would be hard to imagine anyone being able to blackmail Mr. Strauss-Kahn, given the number of parties he attended with the rich and famous in France. His case, in New York, ultimately broke down in court because the victim had a phone call to a man convicted of having 400 pounds of marijuana in his possession and the phone call was recorded, as all such things are, when a person is in jail. Prisoners have fewer secrets than the rest of us. She asked about the wisdom of continuing a case against Strauss-Kahn. He had been one of several people who had deposited up to $100,000 in this woman's bank account, at various times, for what, nobody knows.[64] Eventually, this case fades away and the prisoner is allowed to escape everyone but his wife.

We have since found out who the people in the FBI were who made all these phone calls to their Congressmen, but not what was motivating them to destroy the career of one of the better Generals we have had in the Army. Sex secrets are ones that cannot be let out, and they must have known it. The FBI will find it difficult to sanction a person from telling their Congressional leaders about the affair, because it would look like retaliation for whistle-blowing, even though there is good reason to see this as something else. In the end, Mr. Petraeus will also be left to prosecution by his wife.

None of these people can come close to a sitting President, Bill Clinton, and his lack of common sense in his affair with Monica Lewinsky, but they all have something in common. Like the incoming Chief Executive Officer of Lockheed Martin, Christopher Kubasik, the former CEO of Boeing, Harry Stonecipher, and the founder of Best Buy, Brian Dunn, they were all having "close personal relationships" with someone who wasn't their wife[65], and they all got caught. The essentials of a secret lie in keeping it for as long as it is needed, and none of these people could. It is a measure of the difficulty of keeping this type of secret. They thought they could but this always boils down to a question of fact: did they or didn't they keep it secret? I mention this only because Karlyn Bowman, *Just How Many Spouses Cheat?*, [Forbes On-Line Magazine, 29 June, 2009] says 3-4% of the married population is having an affair right now. They should probably know how to keep a secret.

But, these kinds of cases add another element: could they be blackmailed for what they did? Not likely, or necessary.

When we think of blackmail, we usually think of some idiot who really thinks it is possible to extort money from a person who would like to keep something secret, in exchange for keeping quiet about that thing. Legally, that is close. Blackmail is itself a secret relationship between two, or more parties. David Letterman gets to join the club on this one, but not because he was blackmailed. He was having one of those close personal relationships with someone not his wife, when Robert "Joe" Halderman, a former CBS producer, decided to ask for $2 million to keep quiet about it. Letterman gave this information to his lawyer and his lawyer arranged to pay the money and have Halderman arrested. Letterman announced the whole thing on national television. By doing that, he wasn't going to get blackmailed for it again any time soon. And, here you have at least part of the answer to keeping something a secret. He has to face his wife, but not blackmail.

When there is no longer any point to it being a secret, it takes more energy and business reputation to keep it one, than the person will get back in the end.[66] This general statement about sexual relationships applies equally to National Security and business secrets. We keep a lot of secrets that are far from secret to anyone.

Where it affects our National Security is having people who might be subject to subtle manipulation, when they are involved with someone who is not their spouse. They are caught in a situation where keeping the secret gets harder. They keep things going longer than they should, even after it is known. David Letterman got it right. I remember the press playing over and over President Clinton's public statement that "I have not had sex with that woman, Monica Lewinski", and wondering why the White House Staff had moved Monica out of the White House if nobody knew what was going on between them. They all knew, and that is a risk to our National Security. It usually isn't going to be used directly by an individual who tries to make money from it, but that is not the way governments work. They can be more subtle, and get to know Monica much better than the ever wanted, or needed to. They read her mail and listen to her phone calls. The Chinese hacked the e-mail accounts of almost everyone associated with past elections and probably did the same thing in this one. They would use their knowledge to influence someone like Monica, not by blackmail, but by being nice. They would want to help her to get leverage on the President. That risk applies equally to all the others mentioned here, and anyone who does this sort of thing. It is a hard secret to keep, and an easy one to keep too long.

Paula Broadwell and General Petraeus both had a secret about their relationship. If they had both kept it, it would still be a secret. I don't know or care about the games that were taking place between Mrs. Broadwell and her "friends", nor does it matter to the issue. Nobody else had to know, or even suspect that there was anything between them. The FBI cannot go snooping into people's homes or computer records without having some evidence that a crime had been committed. That suspicion led them to the relationship. The keeping of the various secrets turned out to be too hard to do.

There is no reason for the FBI to get off clean on this either, since one of its agents apparently called his Congressman to complain about how the investigation was going. Once it was no longer a secret, and the cards were played between Congress and the FBI, it was not going to be a secret anymore. When he called them, he should have known what the result would be. He was an experienced FBI agent, not a kid who had just finished the Academy. This is not about the morality or legality of two married people having an affair. It appears, from the press reports, that the FBI had already determined that it was not a national security issue, and may have even been prepared to drop the whole thing, until Congress got involved. That is an organizational decision for the FBI and the Justice Department, not a personal one. Was the FBI agent like W. Mark Felt in Watergate? That is a question you have to answer for yourself.

Mr. Strauss-Kahn, and his maid, also had a secret and the keeping of it might have helped both of them, as it turned out. Nobody will ever know what the nature of this secret actually was. Her lack of credibility made her story of sexual assault sound less plausible. His story of consensual sex was equally hard to believe, and exposed him to the pack of reporters who followed him around afterwards. It gets harder to keep secrets with reporters all over the path you take to work.

The lesson for everyone is keeping secrets is much harder to do than anyone wants to admit. Even when it is clearly in their own interest, people are compelled to act as if it will not matter if one more person knows. The best advice is to think first. There are clear limits on who should have a secret if it is going to be kept.

55 Dylan Byers, Broadwell's co-author to publish WaPo piece, Politico, November 12, 2012

http://www.politico.com/blogs/media/2012/11/broadwells-coauthor-to-publish-wapo-piece-149316.html

56 CIA Website https://www.cia.gov/offices-of-cia/clandestine-service/our-mission.html

57 Jim Dwyer, William K. Rashbaum, John Eligon, Strauss-Kahn Prosecution Said to Be Near Collapse, 30 June 2011 http://www.nytimes.com/2011/07/01/nyregion/strauss-kahn-case-seen-as-in-jeopardy.html?pagewanted=all

58 Staff Writer (unnamed), *John Edwards*, New York Times, updated 13 June 2012, http://topics.nytimes.com/top/reference/timestopics/people/e/john_edwards/index.html

59 Sharon Waxman, The Sex Parties of France's DSK: 'Eyes Wide Shut' Comes to Life, The Wrap, 15 October 2012 http://www.thewrap.com/movies/column-post/sex-parties-france-s-dsk-eyes-wide-shut-comes-life-60641

60 Pascal Rossignol, *France's Strauss Kahn under Investigation in Pimping Case*, Reuters, 26 March 2012, http://www.reuters.com/article/2012/03/26/us-france-strausskahn-investigation-idUSBRE82P11U20120326

61 NBC News, *FBI Agent Sent Shirtless Photo to Kelley before email Investigation, Officials Say* 13 November 2012, http://usnews.nbcnews.com/_news/2012/11/13/15140764-fbi-agent-sent-shirtless-photo-to-kelley-before-email-investigation-officials-say?lite

62 Chris Cuomo, *Rep. Anthony Weiner: 'The Picture Was of Me and I Sent It'* , 6 June 2011, http://abcnews.go.com/Politics/rep-anthony-weiner-picture/story?id=13774605#.UKO3MOOe87A

63 Washington Wire Staff Writer, *Timeline of the Petraeus Scandal*, Wall Street Journal, 13 November 2012 http://blogs.wsj.com/washwire/2012/11/13/timeline-of-the-petraeus-scandal/?KEYWORDS=Petraeus+timeline

64 Jim Dwyer, William K. Rashbaum and John Eligon, *Strauss-Kahn Prosecution Said to Be Near Collapse*, New York times, 20 June, 2011, http://www.nytimes.com/2011/07/01/nyregion/strauss-kahn-case-seen-as-in-jeopardy.html?pagewanted=all&_r=1&

65 Jeff Green, Bloomberg News, *Sex-Scandal CEOs Spark Debate on What's Different in the C-Suite*, the San Francisco Chronicle, Nov 13 2012, http://origin-www.bloomberg.com/apps/news?pid=conewsstory&tkr=LMT: US&sid=aIBfEY3StNss

66 Lawyers.com, Blackmail Costs More than it Pays, accessed 14 November 2012, http://criminal.lawyers.com/Criminal-Law-Basics/Blackmail-Costs-More-Than-it-Pays.html

CHAPTER 7

Secrets Between Friends

When our Armies went into Afghanistan, they faced a new enemy with an old secret. Because we seem to have an inability to teach, or learn lessons from history, our soldiers have to fight the same wars over and over. It isn't just the U.S. that has been involved there.

Afghanistan has been in a war with someone since the early 1800's and it has been almost constant.[67] That isn't even a secret. The British have been there off and on, since before 1838. They suffered horrific casualties, by today's standards of war, and left, only to return in 1878. That time they won, just as they did the first time around – temporarily. The leaders moved in and out of power and finally declared themselves independent of the British Empire. Even that did not last very long, and in 1933 they got a king, with a monarchy in power for 20 years. More confusion is evident until 1973, when the Russians get involved, supporting one government or another, until they invade Afghanistan to make sure things go the way they thought they should. Of course, we know that did not work out well for them, and not much better for us. The U.S. Russia, and Great Britain have all learned to leave Afghanistan with little grace, but more resolve. The secret of Afghanistan is its reluctance to act like a country.

I interviewed an Afghan merchant who travelled all over Afghanistan during most of the war with Russia, the Taliban takeover, and the U.S. involvement. He had an observation that was interesting, and related to his part of the world. He said, "Every big country has a dog. They feed it; they take care of it; they walk it. But, they try not to let their dog attack other dogs or dig holes in the neighbors yard. China has North Korea and Burma [he still used the old name for Myanmar] and Russia has Iran and Syria. If you see problems coming from them, there is a reason and it always comes back to the owner of the dog." His analogy reaches into the way Afghanistan has avoided being at war, while winning every one they have had. They are nobody's dog.

This is not a national army defeating a foreign invasion. It is some tribes banding together with their own armies to defeat one. Each of the tribes has their own, armed militias and they fight because someone, who keeps them employed, wants them to. They have been doing it for a long time because the Afghans make a living of war, and it is a living they do not want to give up.

It is not just the standing militias and private guards. There are government officials, police, rescue workers, hospitals and service workers who depend on one war or another for their living. Of the $6.7 billion we spend, every month, on this war, a percentage goes to local labor for various humanitarian programs, fuel, transportation, schools, and other types of support. We recently had to pay over $600 a gallon for fuel when our friends in Pakistan closed off the border and allowed some terrorists to blow up more fuel trucks. They have done this more than a few times when they get perturbed at us. We give Pakistan over $2 billion a year in military and economic aid, and screamed like banshees when we withheld $700 million to get them to enforce their borders. Yet, we seem to remember the whining, described by Christiane Amanpour, ABC News, as being broadcast by the "usual suspects", more than the public support among foreign leaders. It got a lot louder when the S.E.A.L Team 6 went into Abbottabad, Pakistan, to kill Osama bin Laden. [68]

In Afghanistan, we have difficulty finding out who are friends are, so we can fight our enemies. Part of the secret of war is understanding who the enemy is, but ask almost anyone who our enemies are, and they hesitate. In such an open world, it should be easy to figure out, but it seems to be a kind of secret.

Al Qaeda is a dead giveaway because they advertise on websites and they are not very subtle. They threaten anyone who tries to stop them. You don't have to guess with them, but few are like that. Some of our enemies admit to it, but most do not. They keep parts of their thoughts secret.

Al Qaeda, which does not, is an organization that cannot exist by itself. It isn't a country, a government of any kind, or a thing that can generate taxes to provide services to people it favors. It operates more like Afghanistan, with local tribes who work for money and getting to heaven on a fast track. It seems to be an organization of bomb makers, shooters, and killers that would be favored almost no place we could find. Yet, we know where they are by the body count.

The current administration has had over 300 airstrikes in Pakistan, most of them directed at somebody in Al Qaeda.[69] After Bin Laden was killed, a drone strike got Atiyah Abd al-Rahman, a Libyan who in the last year had taken over as Al Qaeda's top operational planner. The militant leader, Mustafa Abu al-Yazid, an Egyptian, was a top financial chief for Al Qaeda as well as one of the group's founders, and was considered by American intelligence officials to be the organization's No. 3 leader, behind Osama bin Laden and his deputy Ayman Al-Zawahri, another Egyptian. Yazid was killed on May 22 in a drone attack in North Waziristan, a senior Pakistani intelligence official said…. The official said he was in the village of Boya, about 16 miles along a dirt trail west from Miranshah, the main town in North Waziristan, when the missile hit him. Yazid was considered to be the overall commander for al Qaeda for Afghanistan and Pakistan[70]. In December 2012, a drone strike near Miran Shah in North Waziristan killed Sheikh Khalid bin Abdel Rehman, who also went by the code name Abu Zaid al-Kuwaiti. Three days later, three more people are killed by a drone strike in the village of Tabbi, not far away.[71]

Go to your favorite mapping program and search for **Federally Administered Tribal Areas, Pakistan.** Most of the seniors in al Qaeda are in Pakistan, and die in what Google sees as a pink area of this map, in the North-West part of the country. Jalalabad, where the British were going with their contractors, when they were massacred by tribes, is north. Kashmir, where the Indians and Pakistan have had long running arguments leading to fighting, is east. It is not a good neighborhood to live in, unless you want to fight someone. Everyone is doing it.

So, do we think of Pakistan as an enemy of ours because so many terrorists live there? No, we don't. We call them an ally, partner, and fellow combatant against al Qaeda and al Qaeda apparently thinks about them the same way. They blow up a few places in Pakistan to show their displeasure, and ambush troops that are sent in to clear them out. They even kill politicians, as they did in the elections of 2013. You could imagine how we might feel about them killing some of our Mayors, Governors or Congressmen but that is what they are doing in Pakistan. It is hard to believe that so many of them can live there, so unloved, but we should remember that Al Capone lived in Chicago for nine years before the government finally put a team together that could get him. They didn't put him in jail for the killings, extortion, bootlegging, or prostitution that he was really good at. They got him for tax evasion.

Al was a terrorist who learned his trade well. He had plenty of cash from liquor sales to keep him going. He paid off the politicians and police and killed ones who got in the way. He may have learned that from the mob, but it sure sounds a lot like the Taliban or al Qaeda. Like-minded people will tolerate the bad things he did for the benefits he gave. So who would do that for al Qaeda?

Al Qaeda has some resources it has gotten by kidnapping mostly Pakistanis, but the evidence suggests this was a recent development and was not what they did to get started.[72] Where they got their startup financing seems to be a secret, citing "donations", though prior to September 11, they were from Saudi Arabia and a host of imams collecting money for them[73]. The Saudi's deny they were ever involved in any such thing. Since al Qaeda financial leadership has been killed, now and again, it makes collecting and distributing money a dangerous profession that nobody is talking about. But, somebody is still funding their operations, the Taliban in Afghanistan, and a few other trouble-makers around the world, especially in Sub-Sahara Africa. To find the money, we usually have to find the benefit to keeping terrorists employed. That wouldn't be any of our friends. This is an area of secrets that friends try to ignore, but should probably pay more attention to.

The month before the Russians first went into Afghanistan, in December 1979, the Iranians took hostages in our embassy in Tehran, taking the attention of the whole world off everything else for 444 days. We have not been friends with Iran since then, but we weren't friends with them long before that. President Carter had signed a finding, in July, to have the CIA intervene in Afghanistan. The Russians were concerned that the CIA was involved there, though it was a good question about whether they knew about the finding, there was no question that the KGB knew they were there. The CIA knew the Russians were there since several of their military advisors were executed in Herat a few months before.[74] When the Russians invaded Afghanistan, the Iranians started doing the same things to them they had done to the U.S, attacking their embassy, harassing their business interests, and shutting off supplies of gas, which Russia didn't need anyway. They didn't get to be fast friends until the Russians left Afghanistan, not to return. This is the way of friendships in the Middle East. There are ups and downs.

In Afghanistan, we pay for everything and get almost nothing in return. The Russians, during their time there, at least got oil and natural gas for their efforts, while having a sizeable trade imbalance in their favor. They are clever and they only spent, by one declassified CIA estimate, about $50 billion for the entire seven years of war.

Today there are almost 250,000 troops in the Afghan army, most of them equipped and trained by the Allies of NATO. We left an army in Iraq of 350,000, so between them, they have one of the larger armies in the Middle East. [Turkey, which is the second largest in NATO is 800,000.] In both countries, there are police, special security details, guards of all kinds, trade workers of various types, interpreters, drivers, and even spies on the payroll. There may be an equal number of people, maybe more, on the Taliban payroll doing the same kinds of things. It is expensive to run a war like this, but it is part of the business of war.

The Russians are involved in Chechnya, and that is not going much better than Afghanistan. We got small glimpses of it in attacks on Moscow that we seem to have forgotten about. The Russians haven't forgotten. In 2004, two people got on the Moscow subway with bombs and tore apart a train car, killing 39 people and wounding 129.[75] In 2011, 35 people were killed at the Moscow Domodedovo airport, Moscow's busiest.[76] Russia says they came from the same area of the country that our Boston Marathon bombers were from, so they probably weren't too surprised.

The rebels are, today, having trouble getting enough money to operate. In better times, they relied on a smattering of Chechnya's business community, and Islamic charities in the Middle East,

Jordan and, strangely enough, the U.S. to survive. [77] The Russians seem to have been able to choke off some of these resources and have forced the terrorism into lower cost operations like kidnapping and taking school children hostage. These kinds of things don't endear the rebels to anyone in the civilized world and makes getting money even harder. Most of the countries of the West do the same things to al Qaeda, with varied success.

The point of this financial clamp-down is a recognition that money keeps them going, and cutting off the flow of money helps to slow things down. It seems like well-meaning people everywhere would want to do this, but we don't seem to have discovered who is behind this funding. That is the Big Secret. Do we not want to say, or don't we know? It explains who our enemies might be, so we might want to find out who that is.

Aside from a very few sources, there is not much written about terrorist financing, but most of it points back to Iran, Saudi Arabia and private donors doing good deeds for Islamic charities. [78] It is hard to make the Saudis our enemies, any way you look at it and the charities are splintered into groups of people trying to help those Syrian refugees in Turkey, without spilling any of that loose change to the Kurdistan Workers Party (PKK) which the British Foreign Office warns travelers about. According to those warnings, they kidnap people and blow up public areas where tourists may wander. Is doesn't appear that the PKK gets included in the Islamic charities handouts, but nobody knows for sure. Maybe they just aren't saying. That leaves Iran.

There is almost nobody that thinks Iran is a friend of ours, or for that matter, of too many other countries. The Saudis and Iran have been at odds over religious matters for ages and Iraq fought a war with them for eight years [79] that borders on being one of the nasty wars of modern times, though that is hard to qualify, given some of the things that have happened in places like Bosnia and Sudan. But it was nice to see the French supporting Iraq and engaged with the Ayatollah Ruhollah Khomeini who promised to never forget what they did. Another Great Satan in the world gives us some comfort.

So, we might ask ourselves who is benefiting from having terrorists causing trouble in the world's countries? The Russians have had their share of it with the operations in Chechnya, so they don't get much benefit from having terrorism get a boost from anyone. If we were looking for countries that benefited from this kind of thing, we would say that nobody benefits. If that were true, there would be no terrorists anywhere because nobody would pay to keep them going. Somebody does, but that seems to be a secret we have not yet discovered. Or, it is a secret nobody wants to talk about.

In the post-9/11 clean-up of investigative strings, Congress wondered why terrorists financing did not get better attention from the government organizations responsible for keeping an eye on terrorism. In Lee Hamilton's testimony[80], there were reasons enough: The FBI investigated but did nothing to pursue those involved; Justice did nothing in the way of prosecutions; the Intelligence Community had little understanding of how some of these financing operations actually worked; the mixing of legitimate funding and al Qaeda funding was difficult to detect and act on. On the matter of Saudi Arabia, he said:

> "The conclusion was that we found no evidence, as you have stated correctly, that the Saudi Government as an institution or as individual senior officials of the Saudi Government supported al Qaeda. Now we sent investigators to Saudi Arabia. We reviewed all kinds of information and documents with regard to that that are available in the intelligence community. We listened to many, many people who talked to us about these things. We followed every lead that we could....

We did find in this, the pre-attack period, pre-Saudi Arabia attack period, that there was a real failure to conduct oversight in the Saudi Government, there was a lack of awareness of the problem, and a lot of financing activity we think flourished. We think that Saudi cooperation was ambivalent and selective, and we were not entirely pleased with it."

So, are the Saudis our enemies or friends? Probably neither.

China and Russia are Iran's best friends, so they probably know what Iran has been up to and tolerate it. You now have to decide if the friend of my enemy can be my friend. You might have to read that again to understand it. The old Arab saying is *the Enemy of my Enemy is my Friend*, not the other way around. In 2001, the French Ambassador to London said "that shitty little country, Israel" caused most of the trouble in the world[81], so it may depend on who you talk to about this. This less than diplomatic uttering just means different people have different perceptions about who causes trouble, and a good many of them think the U.S. is included in there with Israel. We seem to be confused about this very simple concept. Who is our enemy? It can't be a secret.

In every war, there are friends, neutrals and parties to the conflict. Countries that are not friends, or neutrals, are enemies. Pakistan is a friend of ours, but most of the drone strikes that kill terrorists strike there. We would have to be deaf and blind to believe that having them live there was being a friend to the United States. That, alone, could be a reason for saying they are an enemy.

This is not State Department reasoning. The State Department thinks every country is a friend and ignores the obvious references to things that might be counter to that idea. They would argue that Pakistan cannot possibly control all the border areas of their country and when they tried, the Taliban shot up their army and captured a few of them. They even make excuses for why we might be misinterpreting something we see as unfriendly. It is better to ignore this kind of reasoning and focus on behavior. Some behavioral things are easier to see than others.

A country that says it wants to launch a nuclear weapon on a missile to hit the U.S. is in the enemy camp. That puts North Korea on the top of the list of our least favored nation, but it might surprise you that Pakistan, Iran and North Korea have some areas in common when it comes to nuclear weapons.

What we can't ignore is the North Korea testing of missiles that can reach Alaska and Hawaii, parts of the United States. We know they have tested nuclear weapons. If they can put those two together, they could carry out that threat, but whether they *can* do that is subject to speculation. [82]

Sixty-seven percent of North Korea's trade is with China, and twenty percent was with South Korea. After the North shelled the Yeonpyeong Island and sank one of their destroyers, killing 46 crew members, the South decided to end most of their trade with them. So did Japan. You could hardly blame them. When it comes to sinking some other countries warships, no country is going to take that well.

What we find hard to believe is that China would be offended by anything North Korea did. It seems like they would find it amusing and beneficial to have us over-reacting to the things this little crazy country came up with. What China gets from this is the ability to watch how the free world, specifically the United States, reacts to these threats. They can say how upset they are with their southern neighbors, and even suggest they will cooperate with U.N. sanctions, but they certainly have control that nobody else has.[83]

"The chief rival to this viewpoint holds that China is being duplicitous on the North Korea question and insincere in its statements supporting a freeze or dismantlement of North

Korea's nuclear weapons program. According to this view, Beijing actually has substantial leverage with Pyongyang but elects not to use it in order to ensure that the North Korean issue continues to complicate U.S. regional strategy and undermine the U.S. position in Asia. This is the reason that China appears casually tolerant of North Korea's erratic and unpredictable behavior, why Beijing rarely criticizes North Korea for its provocations, and why Beijing has sided so often with the North Korean position in the Six Party Talks. Furthermore, these proponents suggest that Beijing and Pyongyang actually may be coordinating their policies on North Korea's nuclear weapons program, including the timing of North Korea's more provocative pronouncements and actions, in an effort to keep the United States off balance."

China-North Korea Relations, Congressional Research Office

They cut their oil exports to the North to zero in February of 2013, as a "possible signal" that they were not happy with their neighbors. North Korea could not survive a week without some help from China, but the more they threaten the United States, the warmer the Cold War becomes. North Korea is not going to attack the U.S. but gets a pat on the back from every third world country that thinks throwing stones at the world's biggest superpower is a fun thing to do. More than that, they get a reaction that China and Russia can watch.

A country that calls us the Great Satan and actually helps other countries kill our soldiers and diplomats is an enemy. Iran is not a country I would want on my border, since it says it wants to develop peaceful uses of atomic energy, but thinks it needs weapons grade materials to do that. It has the biggest bunch of religious fanatics the world has ever seen, and they run the country. Iran is an enemy; they say so, and act like it. For those who saw the movie *Argo*, it brings back a time in 1979, when the Iranians captured Americans from the U.S. Embassy and kept them for over a year. Things have pretty much gone downhill from there.

The Iranians want to make nuclear weapons, at least partly because they see what Pakistan, India, Israel and North Korea managed to do with them. Surprisingly few countries have them [see the *Federation of American Scientists* estimates on the numbers at http://www.fas.org/programs/ssp/nukes/nuclearweapons/nukestatus.html] and none of them have very many compared to Russia and the United States. Most countries do not admit to having more than one, so FAS is just guessing when they say what they think each country might have. It doesn't take many to make an impression a neighbor who wants to push up the stakes on a border dispute, or threaten to pop one off over the U.S.

Pakistan has probably done the most for Iran in getting a nuclear weapon. So, when we start to describe behaviors of our potential enemies, giving nuclear technology to an enemy of ours, might be something we should consider. Abdul Qadeer Khan, a prominent nuclear scientist, often accused of spreading his knowledge around the Middle East, says the Iranians tried to buy a nuclear weapon from Pakistan in the 1980s.[84]

The Washington Post story says Pakistan declined to sell them one, but gave them bomb-related drawings, parts for centrifuges to purify uranium and a secret worldwide list of suppliers. "Iran's centrifuges, which are viewed as building blocks for a nuclear arsenal, are largely based on models and designs obtained from Pakistan," the article says. The Iranians say they are only using these centrifuges for building up nuclear material they can use to generate electricity. If that was the case, they wouldn't have needed a bomb. Kahn is claiming senior military officers in Pakistan, possibly some political officials, knew about what he was doing and encouraged it. When Iran asked for a bomb, they were told they could have one, but only if they built it themselves. They certainly seem to be moving in that direction.

More than that, Kahn's list of customers included North Korea, Iraq, and Libya. He was selling technology and access to a privately constructed list of suppliers of it. These suppliers were not ones to ask questions about the intended use of the items they were selling. He put together firms in South Africa, Malaysia, and Turkey to help with manufacturing. Kahn's story that the government was cooperating, may not be true, in which case the nuclear technology was being transferred without their knowledge or consent. We would be equally concerned about Pakistan's ability to protect their own technology as we might be that the cooperated in the transfers. Neither is a good thing.

Among ourselves, we can say that we don't have many enemies in the world, but it is because we take a politically correct view, when that can be our end. Maybe we should take a second thought about who our friends might be.

Diversions in Secrets

We have a mistaken belief that the truth will make us free. Today, a tour stop on a visit to East Asia can now include a torture chamber of the Khmer Rouge in Phnom Penh where almost 20,000 people were routinely beaten to death with iron bars, pickaxes, machetes and makeshift weapons, necessary because, their website says, "the price of ammunition was so high" [85]. Across the country, the Khmer Rouge killed over a million and a half people. They would have killed more, but the country was not that big. Not many High Schools talk about Cambodia, but some students have seen the Killing Fields, and know what happened there; some don't. It would not be surprising to find out students didn't even know where Cambodia is, but that is ignorance and not keeping secrets. It surely wouldn't be on many lists of places to tour, but what they did to their own people is not a secret either.

Cambodia can't even come close to the six million Jews killed by the Nazi in World War II and 1,400,000 people visit Auschwitz-Birkenau every year. Each visit is a reminder of what happened there. In spite of volumes of information, we can still hear someone like Majmoud Ahadinejad deny that any such thing ever happened, and he isn't the only one doing it. There is a website that offers help at http://www.holocaustdenier.com/. Denial is almost a mantra in the world of secret keeping, but Cambodia and Auschwitz are not among those easily denied.

These are things that are far from being secrets, but it seems to take this kind of reminder to maintain an idea so terrible, especially when there are people who deny it. Even with the worst of events, the moments fade away over time. Museums remind us, and our family members, so we can remember. They make it real for people who weren't alive when it happened, and they keep the event current. These are things that are public knowledge when they happen, but fade to secret when time passes.

There is a category of secrets below the big ones that most of us know about. They have been secrets we don't remember, not because we are not very well informed, because we wanted to forget. The National Archives has some pictures that most people do not want to see, but they are not secrets. They are just things we don't want to know. Sometimes, they are just the unexpected.

When I was in the Intelligence business, my son went to Bosnia to work near the Russian border. It was a dangerous place to be, so I would read the intelligence summaries every morning to see what was going on there. One day, some women had killed an American soldier by beating him to death and the details of that report stuck in my mind. It was not hard to imagine my son in that situation. I held onto the briefing book and didn't put it down, long reading what I was there to see. My boss, who was an experienced CIA-trained manager came by and glanced at the top of the page. He stopped and said, "Your son is in Bosnia, isn't he?"

"Yes, sir" I said not really thinking much about the question.

He reached down and took the book out of my hand and put it back on the briefing table. He put his hand on my arm and very gentle said, "You are not to look at this book again until he comes back home", then turned to his secretary and said, "Take him off the access list for the briefing book until I say to put him back on." Some things are better kept as secrets, even from those allowed to see them.

When I was in graduate school, our class of policemen got to interview a prison psychiatrist who had quite a few famous cases, including the Birdman of Alcatraz, who, he told us, tried to hit him across the side of the head with a metal pitcher of water. He treated patients who were criminally insane and none of us had much experience with a class of people like that. He started to go over some of the cases, one-by-one to give us an idea of the wing we had just toured. It looked the same as any other prison, but there was something different about the prisoners. Unlike the normal prison population, these looked like folks you could have lunch with, and live. They took us to a women's prison and I learned a lot there about what to say to embarrass a bunch of male policemen who might be passing through. They thought it was good sport.

He came to the case of a woman who was gentle as a lamb but they kept her behind a partition in her own cell. She seemed to hide behind it, almost out of sight until everyone had gone. He said she was a murderer and that surprised us a little. We had seen plenty of killers that day and she didn't look like any of them. Most of these killers had muscles and tattoos and were not the kind of people you would want to run into on a dark night.

She certainly didn't look like a person who could kill. But, we were not prepared for what came next: she had killed, then eaten, her two children. The breath went out of me and I found myself thinking that such a terrible person must be executed, and not running around alive. It was an irrational thing to think, especially for one in law enforcement, but justice is not well defined for the type of act committed. Nobody in that room had ever heard of such a case, nor of this woman, and four of us lived in the state where she was convicted. No public announcements were made because she was mentally ill and never went to trial.

I asked the psychiatrist how he treated such a person, how he sat across from her and tried to help her, knowing what she had done. I added, "I certainly couldn't do that."

He said, "Of course you couldn't, but it is my job to treat people like her. They pay me over $80,000 a year [a 1970's salary] to sit with these people and try to figure out if they can be helped. So, while you make less than half that amount on your police salary, they pay us a good deal more to deal with these kinds of people. You can't do it, and you shouldn't have to. People like them can't help what they do. They don't think about how other people are going to look at it; they just do it. Where we can, we keep what they did inside these walls. There are awful things you will never hear anything about. Usually, people don't want to know about them." I later found the same type of thing occurs in mental hospitals, where non-criminals are housed with diseases that disfigure or incapacitate them and they are rarely seen by anyone. The visitor rooms are empty. They are horrific creatures who no longer exist outside the walls of the institution.

Early in February, 2013, a young couple, Monica Quan and Keith Lawrence, pulled into their parking slot at their condo in Irvine California, "America's Safest City" and were shot multiple times. Both died at the scene. There were no witnesses; nobody heard gunshots, and the local police were looking for leads. The girls father was Randal Quan, who was called a few days later by a person claiming to be Christopher Dorner and telling Quan he should have done a better job of protecting his daughter. [86] Randal Quan represented Dorner at a disciplinary hearing that lead to his dismissal. Police found a long, winding "manifesto" that names people he held grudges against for various reasons. They set up protection for some of them. A few days later, Dorner is seen by police near one of these potential victims and there is a shootout. Dorner gets away and sees a police cruiser at a stoplight, shoots a young officer to death and drives away. Dorner is eventually surrounded in a cabin at Big Bear Lake, and killed, most all captured by live television. The secret wasn't in what Dorner did, because crimes and death were live and in color. The secret was that most readers of that particular story blamed the LAPD for what happened.[87] Dorner was pushed into it, they said.

While we can debate whether this one murderer was pulled or pushed by any of the events that preceded his death, the nature of his crime is calculating and intentional. It seems illogical that anyone could believe the police were at fault, but they reopened the examination of his misconduct before it was over. His manifesto accused them of racial prejudice, and other things, that opened old wounds. The real secrets sometimes lie below the understanding of crimes committed, and swirl around in motives and suspects unnamed.

He set out to get revenge for a perceived wrong, wrote about why he did it, and died before he could have a trial. Many of his secrets died with him. Compared to the secrets of National Security, the secrets beneath the bodies of the victims are easy to keep. We don't like to think about them. In the words of Al Gore, they are inconvenient truths, hard to think about.

We have the same kind of truth south of us. Mexico has developed a culture of violence that is mind-numbing and very close. Done in the name of claiming a part of a $18-29 Billion drug market, the government casualties since 2006 have been greater than the coalition forces in Afghanistan. [88] Once in awhile, we see something of it because the gangs dump decapitated bodies in places that can't be avoided. They know we don't want to know about every single person who is killed this way, or by having holes drilled in his head with a power drill, so they have taken to killing more of them at a time to get some attention. In May of 2012, there were 49 in one month. If you were to ask the average person in the U.S. if Mexico was violent, they would say "of course" but most don't know much more than that. After a time, we put it out of our heads. Sometimes, this forgetfulness works to the advantage of our enemies.

Malala Yousafzai is a nominee for the Nobel Peace Prize, and most people do not even remember what she did to get the nomination. This young girl tried to get other girls to attend school in the Swat Valley of Pakistan. On her website, she says there are 61 million people who don't go to school there. It shouldn't be particularly dangerous to try to get them to go, but this is the part of Pakistan where the Taliban live. In September 2006, Safia Ama Jan, director of Afghanistan's Ministry of Women's Affairs for the Kandahar Province was killed in from of her house because she was in charge of getting girls to go to school and had 1000 of them attending. [89] This is a government official in charge of a function that the Taliban do not approve of; Malala Yousafzai was not. She was a student.

In October of 2012, a Taliban gunman shot her at close range, the bullet passing through her head, neck and shoulder. She was lucky to get to England to have her skull reconstructed and get herself back to some stage of *normal*. Maybe I'm an ignorant American, but I didn't think there were 61 million people not going to school in the whole world, let alone, one part of Pakistan. And, I believed it was out of character for the Taliban to want to kill a young girl who tried to get other people her age to go to school. They blew up schools, shot teachers, and killed government officials, but I hadn't heard about them killing students of that age in such a public way. Mind you, this doesn't make them good people, but it seemed out of character even for these bad ones.

Pakistan's people, at least initially, did not like what happened to her, and neither did the rest of the civilized world. Why is this a surprise? Why are these things not in the newspapers or on television often enough to be in the minds of a few million people? Because they are secrets that don't get talked about. They are secrets that die away.

The Middle East, from Iran to Algeria has enough bombings that make the news every day, that we don't take notice of it. When I lived in England in the 1970's, the IRA and British were fighting and killing someone every day. There was a morning in 1975 when a BBC report on the night before, said the IRA had gone to a local card game and shot the legs of all of the participants as some kind of warning –kneecapping they called it then. A few of my neighbors in the village said that was enough, and started to turn off the BBC news when it was broadcast. They didn't pay any attention to the radio when Ireland was mentioned. Very slowly, after that, the IRA stopped these kinds of attacks, just as the Chechens stopped theirs. The same thing happens to the Middle East where car bombings are so common that the 26 car bombs that killed 79 people in Iraq and wounded hundreds, were ignored when two men with a pressure-cooker bomb killed three people in Boston. [90]

These are the kinds of secrets that we don't need any help with keeping, because we see them and forget them. The Chinese and Russians do their best to not reinforce the event by eliminating it from history. We can see the point of this without agreeing on whether it is a good thing to do. It is a massive task and I can't imagine the type of army it must take to keep up with all the different types of events that would have to be controlled. They can't control all of them.

In those really dramatic events, like 9-11, there is something called "flashbulb memory" that gives us the moment forever. My wife was in the corridor of the Pentagon where the airplane hit and she turned around to see the fire and blast pressure pushing down the corridor towards her and her friend. The circuit breakers were popping, making the lights go out, at the same time the ceiling tiles were falling down from the pressure wave. Fire, darkness around the core, but a lighted corridor overhead seemed not right. That was in her flashbulb memory.

They ran out an exit before it got to the end. Researchers say you can answer the question, "Where were you at the time you learned about this?" and be pretty accurate, though you may be off on the timing of events. My wife remembers it clearly. For the rest of these types of things, forgetting is easy and maybe necessary to keeping good relations with companies, governments, and people who need to get along.

It is hard to sit down with that woman after finding out what she did to her children, but it is just as hard to sit down with a cold-blooded killer who was elected to a leadership office in a Latin American country. In order to deal effectively with him, a person has to push away those secrets and not think about them. Not remembering what we know may be useful, not ignoring those secrets, but suppressing them until the work is done.

---

67 See BBC *Afghanistan Profile*, 31 March 2013, http://www.bbc.co.uk/news/world-south-asia-12024253

68 Peter Bergen, *Who Really Killed Bin Laden?*, CNN World, updated 27 March 2013, http://www.cnn.com/2013/03/26/world/bergen-who-killed-bin-laden

69 Pam Benson, *CNN Fact check: Is al Qaeda's Core Decimated or is Group Growing*, CNN, 23 October 2012. http://www.cnn.com/2012/10/22/politics/fact-check-al-qaeda/index.html

70 Eric Schmitt, *American Strike is said to Kill Top Qaeda Leader*, New York Times, 31 May, 2010, http://www.nytimes.com/2010/06/01/world/asia/01qaeda.html

71 Nasir Habib, Senior al Qaeda leader killed in Pakistan, officials say, CNN, http://www.cnn.com/2012/12/09/world/asia/pakistan-al-qaeda-killed/index.html

72 Associated Press, *Cash-Strapped Al Qaeda Turns to Kidnapping and Ransom to pay Operational Costs*, 19 June, 2011, http://www.foxnews.com/world/2011/06/19/turn-to-kidnapping-showed-bin-ladens-interest/

73 Al Qaeda Funding in Afghanistan, Global Security.Org., http://www.globalsecurity.org/military/world/para/al-qaida-funding.htm

74 Svetlana Savranskaya, (ed), Volume II: Afghanistan: Lessons from the Last War, The National Security Archive,

75 Jill Dougherty, Moskow Metro Blast Kills 39

76 Alexei Anishchuk, Suicide Bomber Kills 35 at Moscow's Biggest Airport, Reuters, 24 January 2011, http://www.reuters.com/article/2011/01/24/us-russia-blast-airport-idUSTRE70N2TQ20110124

77 Associated Press, Chechen Rebels Hurting for Money, September 2004, http://www.foxnews.com/story/0,2933,132617,00.html

78 Matthew Levitt and Michael Jacobson, The Money Trail, Finding, Following and Freezing Terrorist Financing , November 2008

79 http://www.nytimes.com/1981/02/08/weekinreview/the-world-in-summary-in-iran-iraq-war-a-bombing-run-down-memory-lane.html

80 The 9/11 Commission Report: Identifying and Preventing Terrorist Financing, 23 August 2004

81 BBC News, *'Anti-Semitic' French envoy under fire*, 20 December 2001, http://news.bbc.co.uk/2/hi/1721172.stm

82 See BBC, How Potent are North Korea's Threats? 2 April 2013

83 See page 4: China-North Korea Relations, Congressional Research Office, December 28, 2010 http://www.fas.org/sgp/crs/row/R41043.pdf

84 R. Jeffrey Smith and Joby Warrick, *Pakistani Scientist Khan describes Iranian efforts to buy nuclear bombs*, Washington Post, March 14, 2010, and Christopher Clary, *The A. Q. KHAN Network: Causes and Implications*, Naval Post Graduate School, December 2005

85 Website of the Tuol Sleng Museum, Cambodia http://www.tuolslengmuseum.com/History.htm

86 Matt Coker, *Monica Quan, Titans Basketball Coach, and Fiance Keith Lawrence Found Shot to Death*, OC Weekly, 5 Feb 2013

87 See   http://www.dailymail.co.uk/news/article-2276671/Christopher-Dorner-1-million-reward-Killer-cop-called-victims-father-taunt-death.html

88 Michael Kelley, *BY THE NUMBERS: Why The Mexican Drug War Should Keep You Awake At Night, Business Insider,* 18 June 2012: http://www.businessinsider.com/mexican-drug-war-statistics-2012-6#ixzz2RxVjGmXF

89 *The List: The Political Assassinations of 2006,* Foreign Policy, 27 November 2006. http://www.foreignpolicy.com/articles/2006/11/26/the_list_the_political_assassina-tions_of_2006

90 Dirk Adriaensens, Boston on the Tigris, Iraq's Unreported Terror Event, Global Research, 23 April 2013, http://www.globalresearch.ca/boston-on-the-tigris-iraqs-unreported-terror-event-twenty-six-car-bombs/5332627

CHAPTER 8

Lesser Secrets

This is one of the reasons so many business people have very poor memories when they deal with business leaders in other places. Informal secrets abound and many of them are not more than unsubstantiated rumor, compared to the ones that governments and businesses make. But, when people think of secrets, most think in terms of National Security secrets. What the White House does when it exposes a covert program is damaging to National Security, but these are the highest levels of secrets. Our system of secrets produces a lot more than that.

Our National Security secrets are based on Executive Orders that the President issues. In spite of every President being different, they haven't managed to change the National Security side of secrets very much over the years. The real problem lies in special laws for Atomic Energy, Defense, Tax laws, Patents, Law Enforcement, Privacy types of things, Health Care, Controlled Unclassified, CIA-related, and many other things that someone wants to protect, have been added. Some of these special types of information like nuclear information also have their own names, like Critical Nuclear Design Information (CNWDI), Top Secret Restricted Data or Secret Restricted Data which all come under the Atomic Energy Act. This always makes me wonder how the Chinese got the designs of our nuclear weapons, when the Department of Energy has such good control over all of these special kinds of secrets. There are many different types of combinations of information that can exist, which is confusing for the people who are trying to share information with one another.

We used to call all these special categories, "the secret handshake" for all the briefings that we had to get to see them. I could never remember all the ones I had access to, and couldn't carry around a list of them, because the list would be classified. This makes remembering impossible. If someone asked me if I was briefed on so-and-so program, I would say yes, and write down the designator for it. Then I would go back and asked the people in Security if I had a briefing for it. If I didn't, they would give me one. This isn't the way it is supposed to work, but we had to do what was needed to compensate for a complicated system. There are too many of these for anyone to remember.

This can get even more complicated when a person has access to lots of National Security compartments because they have three-letter designations like ABE. This means it is possible to have Top Secret, Top Secret ABE, or Top Secret CNWDI/ABE or a hundred thousand other combinations of these. It is impossible for the people who work with all of this to remember all these different combinations or what they have been briefed on and it makes briefing charts very confusing to the normal human being. It is just easier to leave everything Top Secret and not have to try to remember all other little things that go with it, but people just won't. The only way some of them can feel special is to have their own little compartment. In spite of all these different types, the Chinese have stolen almost all of our nuclear weapons designs, so compartmenting them is not helping us very much.

Who Says That is Important?

Governments and businesses take an almost opposite approach on how to identify when something is important. For anything to be classified by the government, it has to fall into a few categories of things that are classifiable[91]. Businesses don't have this kind of pseudo-scientific approach, so they don't have normal people making these types of decisions; they have lawyers doing it. Trade secrets, patent protection, funds transfers, and privacy make business very complicated.

The Federal government looks on secret-making as a set of rules governed by people who are trained to make decisions about what is important. This is ridiculous, but at least they have a structure to what they do for National Security related things. Business leaders might consider that the Federal way has some merit because there are a limited number of people making decisions, except in the Army, and they have a purpose of determining what is most important and needs protection.

- The Federal system assumes there will be a person called an original classifier. This is the person who really gets to say something is worthy of protection and how much will be needed. All the Agencies have 2300 of these, but only one was in the CIA[92]. Either the CIA or the agencies with lost of these people have it right, but we can only speculate on which that would be. If the CIA can do it with one person, most medium sized businesses could manage it with one lawyer.

- Second, to make something protected the originator has to have an interest. The information must be owned by, produced by, or under the control of the United States for the Feds to have an interest like this. I have seen contractors refuse to sell a commercial product to the government because they don't want the government to have that kind of interest. The item can then be classified and there is quite a bit of baggage that comes with that. Except by agreement or law, we generally can't control information we don't own, so those interests are important.

°   Businesses and government agencies control a good deal of information by agreement, especially non-disclosure agreements. It is always a good idea to know what kinds of commitments were made to other companies and government entities that affect how much data has to be protected and from whom. Most do not. When I worked for IRS for a short time, I was surprised to find the rules for protecting taxpayer data were pretty stringent, but there was no way, for most people who had it, to know what they were. There were lots of rules but no enforcement.

- Third, for the government the important information has to fall into one of these categories: (a) military plans, weapons systems, or operations; (b) foreign government information; (c) intelligence activities (including special activities), intelligence sources or methods, or cryptology; (d) foreign relations or foreign activities of the United States, including confidential sources; (e) scientific, technological, or economic matters relating to the national security, which includes defense against transnational terrorism; (f) United States Government programs for safeguarding nuclear materials or facilities; (g) vulnerabilities or capabilities of systems, installations, infrastructures, projects, plans, or protection services relating to the national security, which includes defense against transnational terrorism; or (h) the development, production, or use weapons of mass destruction.

Given the subject matter, it is not hard to see that this is pretty serious stuff, but all it really means is that not just anyone in the government can come along and classify just anything. It has to fit into one of the generic categories and the government needs to have an interest. But, it isn't that simple.

Businesses operate almost the same way governments do, using different names to what they want to protect. *Proprietary*, which is a general class that includes copyrighted material, patents, trade secrets, personnel data, and others that more or less relate to the type of business being done. There are secrets about third parties that have nothing to do with the actual conduct of business, but concern who it is done with i.e. their customers, or clients of their customers.

In between these is a class that I would call Court-directed secrecy. Patent secrecy orders fall into this category, but there are, unfortunately, more. As a simple example, there is Grand Jury Information. I have been on both sides of and it, being on a Federal Grand Jury, and protecting Federal Grand Jury information being used in investigations. I'm not saying the rules for this make sense to anyone, but they have been around so long that nobody in government has figured out that they don't make sense anymore.

I was on a Federal Grand Jury, in Virginia, that met for three days every month for eighteen months. We got to hear all the testimony from the various players in the criminal cases that surrounded the investigation of President Clinton and a few other folks that were being looked into. Some people called this the Starr Grand Jury, for Kenneth Starr, the prosecutor. They had warned us not to say anything about the people or events that were being investigated but nobody tried to get any information from any of us, and it was disappointing. We were all hoping for it, so we could jump into action, but we never saw a person with a press pass until the trial actually started. We got to interview witnesses, ask questions, and vote on whether we thought an indictment should be brought against someone. It wasn't until I went to work for the FBI that I found out how Grand Jury Information is protected after it left the Court House and went downtown. It is complicated.

Each Grand Jury has a list of people who are connected with the investigation that can have access to the information that is generated. There were 22 of us on the Jury, so we had access to the information, but there were lawyers on both sides, Judges, court officers, and people like that who were present during testimony, or briefing their clients outside the Grand Jury room. In Virginia, the lawyers were not inside the Jury room when testimony was given, so they only had the word of their client on what was said. We really wanted to know what some of them told their attorneys, because it was not exactly what the newspaper speculation was implying. It was interesting to see the differences.

There were case agents in the various police jurisdictions and FBI that were all involved in some way, but these people had evidence and could not have access to the rest of the case. There is a much smaller list that gets access to all of that. This list is actually made up by the Court and signed by the Federal Judge responsible for the case. Special access lists have to be made by the FBI that correspond to that list, so that only agents assigned to that case and on the Grand Jury list can have access to what it is that case. It is difficult to change the list, so most agents who were on the list, stayed on the cases for a long time. It is more difficult to keep track of all this than you might think.

Each of these steps has to have an equivalent action in a computer to control the access. A file has to have an access control list and anywhere it goes, that list has to apply. That would be fairly easy if there were only one Grand Jury, but there are hundreds of them.

Every State and Federal Grand Jury out there processes cases by the hundreds, so there are going to be just as many access lists. People who retire, leave the FBI, or transfer, have to be accounted for and their access monitored or terminated. Grand Juries come and go and there are quite a few of them. There were four Federal Grand Juries meeting in Virginia each week and in the case of the Starr Grand Juries there were Federal Grand Juries in Washington

D.C. and Maryland hearing evidence in the cases that did not occur in Virginia's jurisdiction. This is just for one case and there are thousands of cases going on in the US at any given time. It creates a type of information that has to be protected and makes work for a few people in government who have to figure out how to protect all the different types of cases as they come and go.

A related kind of information goes with evidence in a criminal trial, or a National Security case. In the latter, some of the evidence may be classified, so lawyers on both sides have to have security clearances to see it. Besides the special court rules for handling classified, there is a whole set of rules called the Federal Rules of Evidence, that cover most of the ins and outs of protecting these kinds of secrets. It is about three-quarters of an inch thick and there is case law on top of that. Law Enforcement material is always interesting because there are orders to a business to allow the tapping of a phone or computer as a part of a criminal investigation or some type of Counter Terrorism under the Patriot Act.

You can imagine the number of these that are conducted every day and all the information that is collected through one of them has to be protected. About 1.3 million requests were made to various cell phone carriers in the U.S. related to wiretaps, physical location, and text messages of various individuals.[93] National Security Letters (NSL), can be used without a warrant and tell the vendor the person is being investigated under the Patriot Act. They cannot speak to anyone except their corporate attorney about what the letter is asking for. The letters are being challenged in court, by some company that is not named, because the name of companies who receive an NSL are secret. *Read that again.* The evidence collected may never end up in a court, but those identities will continue to be a secret.

Sometimes investigators are just asking for the telephone numbers that this person called in time period, other times they are asking for a location of the individual when the call was made. They may already know who was being called. There are another set of wiretap warrants that cover things like wired lines, espionage cases that are classified, Patriot Act warrantless cases, and requests from overseas carriers. We will never know how many of those there are, but there are more than just a few AP reporters involved.

In wiretaps, secrets get very complicated. A wiretap is not very selective about what gets collected, so we have the bank robbery planning and the discussions between the gang member and his wife and girlfriends who are not robbing any banks. Being married and having a girlfriend is not against the law, though what you do with the girlfriend might be. You never know how many people a wiretap will pick up. The person may talk to his Governor or Congressman. The things they are talking about are interesting, but not necessarily criminal. All of the transcripts and audio recordings are still secrets, and some of them may be National Security kinds of secrets.

With counter terrorism cases, there is the added dimension that the intelligence agencies are involved and they are not law enforcement. That is complicated, but not confusing. Intelligence agencies cannot do law enforcement, but they can do law enforcement "support operations", meaning they can help out now and again. You remember that NSA said they had been monitoring terrorists' cell phones overseas? NSA doesn't need a warrant to do that, so they are collecting all kinds of things, like what the terrorist's wife wants him to bring home after work. If the person is a U.S. citizen, they do need a warrant. The food he brings home would not normally be of interest to law enforcement, but NSA might want to know what he is bringing home, especially if they wanted to know where home was. There is always a question about how much, if any of this stuff is allowed to be released to a law enforcement agency. The Intelligence Community can find a person, talk among themselves about what they want to do about him, and go do it, without ever involving law enforcement. When one of those Reapers comes screaming down on a guy in a pickup in the Northwestern corners of Pakistan, he is not going to trial, so the word "evidence" may not be used to describe what has been collected about why he is being killed. It is called a target package.

But, suppose our terrorist is talking to the people who grow poppies in the mountains and we don't like the result of heroin being sent to Europe. Or, even more difficult, supposed we find out our terrorist is talking to an American company about buying some cash sorting machines to speed up processing of his money. The information was collected without a warrant, for National Security reasons. It was never intended to be used in court because that is not why we gather intelligence. It wasn't even collected and maintained by the rules of evidence. Whether NSA could share that with the Drug Enforcement Agency (DEA) is a good question, and the basis for most of the "information sharing" problems between agencies. It is also the reason we used to call NSA "Never Say Anything", which may not be as fair as we thought, back then.

They have their own priorities. By the time they translate all the things they collect in telephone calls, I may be dead, because there are so many of them. An army of translators couldn't keep up. Then, each of the calls requires some analysis, like the cash machines which might be used in a business in downtown Kabul, and not just for sorting drug money. That takes time and resources that nobody has.

The Drug Enforcement people just say, "Give me everything and I will translate and sort through it on my own time." And that sounds reasonable, but it isn't. They couldn't use it in court even if they wanted to and it involves someone in another country where the U.S. doesn't have jurisdiction. Second, NSA might not want DEA knowing where they got the information about who to monitor. That might give up someone's source and it might be an allied source or one of ours. Third, there is always the problem of the drug lord talking to U.S. persons, some of whom may not be involved in any criminal activity. They may sell real estate, teach children, or supply ships for cargo. NSA cannot collect information on U.S. persons, but they have no idea who the terrorist is talking to, where the person might be, or what nationality they are. They might find out after they translate the call, and they might not. Keeping these kinds of secrets is usually a lot more complicated than the average person would believe. Most of the time, they find it easier to not share information because the rules on sharing are difficult. I can't say that I blame them.

There are secrets on top of secrets in law enforcement, and they may need a Task Force just get all the different types of agencies involved that may have an interest. In the Task Force, NSA can have a person look for relevant data on certain types of things and act as the releaser. The Task Forces then create secrets about all the other secrets that have been developed. Then, they can ask that Grand Juries be formed and we can start that process on top of it. All of these secrets have to separated in different cases and only shown to the law enforcement people who are working on them or might need to have them to support one of their own cases. It is a mess and a mess that repeated with the Boston Marathon bombers.

Identifying What is Secret

Once people have decided to protect a particular thing, they have to give guidance to people in their organization about what that thing really is. It is far from simple.

Government people who have to write things that are going to be classified will use "guidance" that will come from an original classification authority and they will make "derivative" classification decisions. Businesses do similar types of guidance especially for patents and trade secrets, which may even have a court order attached, describing what has to be protected. Given a choice, I would rather have a court order. A patent secrecy order says what is part of the patent and gives an order to protect that from other companies that might want to do the same kind of work. You might image how complicated this can be in all the patent litigation cases that are going on in the Samsung and Apple court fight. But, most people never see the guidance that has been issued because it isn't being sent to them, nor is it available to everyone. If everyone could see it, it wouldn't be much of a secret. Both sides are limited on the number of people who know why something was protected or why it wasn't.

A person writing something sensitive is not supposed to decide for himself when something is really a secret; he is supposed to have guidance. This rule is harder to follow, than to say. It is the kind of thing where Oracle might have trouble with all of their suppliers. Who is to say that new chip is only being made for Oracle products? Can anyone remember what products they are not allowed to talk about? Most people make mistakes, but they are supposed to use guidance to keep those mistakes down. Since some places never got around to issuing guidelines, or the guidelines are not current, you can see the dilemma. It is the kind of area where a person can just make things up. We live with these mistakes for a long, long time. Government mistakes are classified for 25 years.

We forget sometimes that secrets are contextual, i.e. they are sensitive in some circumstances but not others. I worked on the President's Critical Infrastructure Protection Committee where we were concerned with things in computer systems that might cause our nation trouble. Every once in awhile, we would have a worm or a Trojan program that would infect all kinds of computers all over the world and cause serious damage. AT&T might report the outbreak of a worm called Ajax. Several of us sitting around the table might say they had seen it too and isolated it, but we called it something different. We might all agree to call it Ajax, since AT&T found it first. Our sharing centers were working on a solution. At the same time, we were getting reports that some government agencies were also getting infected by Ajax.

NSA rolled up these reports into a Top Secret report that said where and how many of these had occurred. We could talk to the press about our problems with Ajax, but we couldn't talk to them about the problems the government agencies were having with Ajax. When they rolled our industry reports into their own, our information became Top Secret. That is the nature of context. Sometimes things are classified and sometimes not, and a person has to remember the hundreds of different things that are and where it was when we saw it. There were different countries involved, different attacks, and many topics besides viruses and worms. It takes thinking about some of the things to remember what was classified and when. This is the kind of thing that reminds me of playing darts. If you are really good, and practice quite a bit, you can get pretty close almost every time. You will slip now and again, but you won't be far off. If you don't play often, you might hit the guy standing at the bar next to the board.

There are events that are sensitive, only until the time they occur, like what Apple is going to talk about at their next developer's conference. They keep it secret right up until the doors are opened and the developers start pushing through. They may get hints and rumors but there is not much available that can be confirmed until the doors open. That takes quite a bit of security to pull off and they do it well. These kinds of things may not be sensitive very long, but there will be plenty of messages, e-mail and things laying around for months afterwards that are still treated as secrets. It takes awhile to get rid of them. Apple must think it is worth that.

The government has this down to an art form, with its guidance being both time and event sensitive. Each program that is formally classified has to have a classification guide for people who are generating information. It may be very detailed and over an inch thick and there is no possible way to remember all the things that are in it. Some classification guides are also classified in their own right, so we have secret guides governing secret development programs, producing secret things. Human nature being what it is, it is easier just to classify everything than trying to sort through what is really classified, and that is exactly what people do. We end up with reams and reams of things that are not really classified but would take a long time to sort through to release them. Nobody wants to sort through them, so they are archived at the end of a program and sit in a computer somewhere forever, or until they reach a magical declassification date where they have to be reviewed. The rules for how to do this are the most convoluted things imaginable, hidden under a nice name, Records Management. This gets very confusing sometimes.

Not all programs ever generate a classification guide and the ones who do can barely keep up with changes that might occur as something is built. The problem with being time and event sensitive is both change quickly and that is hard to keep up with. Given the contextual nature of things, a guide has to change as the product is developed, but that is too hard to do for most programs. This was fine before computers could generate things by the metric ton, but it is just too hard go back to see what has already been marked as classified. The guides tend to be generated and never changed. In a 2010 report to the President[94] only about a third of the guides were updated in the last five years, resulted in a Fundamental Classification Guidance Review program created by President Obama under Executive Order 13526. All Federal agencies with significant classification programs had until July 2012 to review their classification guidance, and then provide summaries of their reviews to the Director of the Information Security Oversight Office[95]. The CIA reviewed its one classification guide, while DoD reviewed the 2070 guides it had prepared. The Justice Department created more classification guides than it got rid of, but had very few to begin with. State, in spite of its problems with Wikileaks cables, did not reduce or change very many of its guides. The inconsistency with the way the Presidential direction was applied, seemed to go unnoticed by the leadership. So, some things that should be formal secrets, never are, and some things that have been secrets, and should not be anymore, are still secrets.

Not everything stays sensitive forever. About half of everything produced by the government will be. Every year, about 30 million pages of text are declassified, but almost that much is created.

Businesses usually don't have any kind of statistics on this, but they will regret not doing a better job of managing data if they get into *discovery* during a lawsuit. In discovery every business will be asking for records surrounding an issue and those will include e-mails, files, and databases on company systems, laptops, home computers if used for business, and interconnected networks. The discovery will cover records management procedures and policies for retention of records of an employee who leaves the company. Of course the more that is available, the more will be available to discovery. The value of information seldom has the respect it is due until someone asks for it, so businesses tend to rid of their information better than the government does.

In June of 2012, in the midst of one of the more interesting patent suits between Samsung and Apple, the judge found that

Samsung had been destroying some of its e-mail as part of its regular purge of e-mail to keep down the volume. Since they had been given notice of discovery in this case, they were supposed to stop destroying material related to the "look and feel" issues between the two companies. Apparently, they didn't. Did they destroy any relevant e-mail? Nobody will ever know unless it pops up somewhere from the guy who had it on his cell phone and went on vacation.[96] It is still out there somewhere, but if they read their email like I read mine, it may take them a month to find out where.

How much is an email worth is it is warning someone in Samsung that they might have made the new phone a little too close to the Apple iPhone? Ask Google, because it was the Google warning to Samsung, that it was a little too close to Apple's design that convinced the jury to award a billion dollar settlement to Apple. I have seen more than a few cases where it was cheaper to take a chance on destroying records than providing them all in discovery, but they will always have to worry that some of those "destroyed" e-mails are always around somewhere. And, of course, they can have legal action against them for doing it.

We will never get ahead of the volume of sensitive things because computers can match anything we try to do and win every time. People in Information Security will tell you there is a records management system for data assigned to every document, so it will not be kept forever. That is a myth. Somebody has to find that document and look at it so it can be released and that is time-consuming. It is easier to just forget about it and let it be, and computers make that easier. It isn't a real document anymore when it is in a computer. It is just a bunch of electrons. I am only kidding, but I have heard that more than once.

Where this becomes very complicated is when we start combining secret things. Combining things is harder. If I am going to build an airplane that is secret, it will have many parts to it that are also secret. It might, e.g. have internal electronics that do special things that are secret, little antennae that are connected to those electronics, black boxes that nobody knows about, special types of metals that are used and thousands of other things. Each one of those is supposed to have its own classification guide and those are all supposed to be lumped into a larger Big Airplane Classification Guide. You can imagine how often that really happens. Even if they had them, they would really be hard to read or remember. A person could do that when there was only paper to be concerned about, but now all the design work is done on computers and moves too fast.

Imagine an agency like CIA, that has thousands of secret things trying to figure out what is a formal secret and what is not. It is too hard to do. It is easier to just classify all of it and make it simple. I don't think they would be stupid for doing things this way; it is just too hard for anyone to figure all this out. They classify first, then concentrate on what to declassify and release, and that is why they only need one classification guide and DoD needs 2000.

Harder than combining secret things, is using something that is not a secret to build something that will be a government secret. If I am making software to do deep mining of data in databases all over the world, a government agency can come along and say, "How about let's use that software to look for things that are secrets. OK by you?" This is not a hard question for most vendors. They may not like what results though. Now the government has an interest and they can classify one of my pieces of software or the process of producing the software that is being sold to the government.

Here, you enter the realm of Industrial Security, which in government parlance is the nether world, like purgatory, where people go before moving on to something better. Businesses get security clearances, so when candidate Romney said, "businesses are people" he was saying legal entities are just like regular folks. Well, sort of, would have been a better response, since universities, businesses, one-person Chapter S corporations, law firms, and various other things can be legal entities. They can act like one being, and they can get a security clearance, just like a person would. It is more complicated, and takes longer, but they can still do it. These are businesses that keep government classified secrets and, at one time, there were 17,000 of them. The government only gives them classified contracts if they have security clearances, but they can't get a security clearance until they have a classified contract. This kind of logic is why I left the government.

---

91 Executive Order 13292, Classified National Security Information, April 2009, page 1.

92 Information Security Oversight Office, 20010 Report to the President, page 3.

93 Julian E. Barnes, *Law Agencies Seek More Data From Cell Carriers*, Wall Street Journal, 9 July 2012 http://online.wsj.com/article/SB10001424052702304022004577515681998852676.html

94 Annual Information Security Oversight Report to the President, http://www.archives.gov/isoo/reports/2010-annual-report.pdf

95 Fundamental Classification Guidance Review, Information Security Oversight Office, http://www.archives.gov/isoo/fcgr/

96 Josh Ong, *US judge rules that Samsung was responsible for deleted emails in Apple patent suit*, The Next Web, 25 July 2012 http://thenextweb.com/apple/2012/07/25/us-judge-rules-that-samsung-was-responsible-for-deleted-emails-in-apple-patent-suit/

CHAPTER 9

Keeping Employees Quiet about Secrets

When bombers blew up a homemade device at the Boston Marathon, two CNN reporters were on the Hill scene waiting for closed session briefings were being held to advise Congressional leaders about what intelligence information might be known about the two individuals. The reporters stood together, talking back and forth, obviously waiting for something. One reporter held up a smart phone and was reading from a message she had just gotten. A person who had just been in that briefing, was telling the reporter what the key elements of the briefing were, in a close a time as can be, given the circumstances.

Our system of secrets tries to work to make sure that any secret worth having is worth keeping quiet about. Just from what my readers have seen so far, I wonder if they believe the system of protecting secrets works very well - anywhere. It is a nice idea, but it doesn't. Employees talk too much, and their talk is an individual decision, not an organizational one. Let me explain this a little.

When most information was kept on paper, it was easy to protect it. It could be kept in locked containers, in locked buildings, and the employees needed to get past guards, locks, and "secretaries" who were tyrants about giving anything to anyone, just to see it. Organizations could make decisions about what was given to whom and how it would be controlled. Some of them still believe they can do that, but they are dreaming.

When it comes to giving out information, the individual gets access to more than anyone ever thought about, and has the power in information technology to give it to most anyone they want. There are places like social media, forums, and business associations where information is routinely shared. There may be consequences to them for the sharing, but only if the employer finds out, and can point to a particular person. So, we have to recognize that most of the methods we have to keep people from talking about secrets don't work very well, because they are really difficult to enforce. It is hard to figure out who actually leaked the information unless it is very specific and known only to a few, or has been planted by someone looking for leaks. More people now can give information away, than when I was growing up in the World of Secrets. There may be a good reason for why they do it.

Unlike most other areas of human interaction, there is not a lot written about keeping secrets. There have been a few studies on secret keeping that give an indication that we are stressed by keeping them. [97] It is a kind of irony that we should be, since it makes some people feel better to know that they have something that not everyone knows. That knowledge can work against us. I can vouch for that because, after awhile, the number of secrets blurs into each other and the line between secret and not-secret gets fuzzy. We have to keep our brains working to keep track of what is secret and what not, and to identify when, and how of secrets can be given up. It is hard work to manage the keeping of secrets[98]. A few people over-react to the stress.

I testified at a hearing for a government contractor who told his employees not to follow policies that were intended to protect secrets in computers. He said the rules were not that important since all of his employees were good people. They were trying too hard and losing focus on their real work that he was paying them for. He wanted to ease that pressure. It sounded plausible and rational to some of the people around him.

Those good people were throwing things in the trash that should have been shredded and throwing computer disks away without getting rid of the information on them. It didn't take long for that to bubble up to us, since the people who picked up the trash in their neighborhood knew what *Secret* meant. When we finished his hearing, I was pretty sure he really believed his employees would not do some of the things they had done. He was surprised that his statements about not following all the rules led to them not following any of them. He thought they had more judgment than that. The Federal government and business sectors are not that trusting.

Almost any employment agreement has a set of clauses that tell an employee they can't take secrets away from the company and go and use those secrets at some other place. The government and private sector, both have them. Both also try to control speaking about secrets in public. In the days when we only went to one company out of college, and stayed there forever, that worked pretty well. But, we don't do that anymore. Now, we might work for four or five companies, and we need to keep those secrets separated. I had trouble remembering where I had been, and when, let alone what secrets I picked up at each place. Consultants travel from place to place and there value comes, in part, from seeing how businesses do a certain function. How they do it may be proprietary to them, but they write press releases about it, have other parts of the company look at the same function, and they share information about it with their partners, sometimes without even knowing they have done it.

Trade Secrets and Proprietary information are tricky because sharing both is required to get work done. Consultants spend a lot of time doing research on open-sourced material that can be shared with other companies, but it is the secret that another business does not know, that gives trade secrets their value. When I dealt with customers of ours, or with partners, I was pretty sure they would protect our secrets because I thought they could be sued in a U.S. court if they didn't. That was probably naive. It becomes murky, the more customers and business partners that are added. For international companies, it is harder still. One day a company is a partner, and the next day the company is a competitor. A person has to ask, "What was it we were working with them on?" It is impossible to keep it straight.

That would be easier if all the secrets were clearly identified, but they aren't. I worked with a number of companies that didn't identify anything as proprietary but wanted us to sign an agreement to say we had a duty to protect anything that was. Almost nobody marked things as proprietary, but all of them required a non-disclosure agreement. We had no idea what we were protecting or couldn't disclose, so we figured we would just protect it all until the work was over. What then?

What we couldn't do was see what our business partners did with that information later, when our cooperation was over. They could use our same approach in a proposal or bid and we would not be any the wiser. We might even lose a bid on a project and never see the competitor's bid, so we would never have an opportunity to find out how they structured it or how much they were going to charge. Unless they used papers that said "Proprietary" on them, nobody would know. The other less obvious part of this is that most bids and proposals are done in a closed business computer system that limits how much of the material that can be taken from it. Not everyone does this, but the bigger companies do. It is probably needed now, more than ever, but IT shops are cutting costs by doing away with these proposal centers and outsourcing the work to subcontractors to prepare bids. These companies work for multiple contractors and that will usually not work out well in the end. The constant interaction of business makes keeping secrets hard.

We seem to believe that we can make agreements and laws that will stop someone from giving up secrets, but never, in history, has that worked. The key to teaching employees about secrets may be to teach them better judgment in identifying and communicating secrets, not how effective the sanctions against them will be, but, that is not the business way. They sue, and so does the government.

My lawyer once told me, while truth is an absolute defense in court, it won't keep you from being sued. If I were in a major bank and knew WIKILEAKS were even thinking about publishing information that I could characterize as "stolen", you can bet I would have lawyers lined up to try to stop it from being published. Litigation is our way, but in fairness to most businesses, they are not focused on suing the little guy in the company who worked there five years ago. They focus their suits because they are expensive to do and have to be worth it in the end. I saw a guy leave a company I worked for and set up a competing business but our company would not sue him. They said it wasn't worth the cost, but cut him off from any association with us. He eventually failed, and went to work somewhere else. Maybe they were right about how to handle it, but it didn't feel right.

NSA got sued because a person claimed they knew about alien visitors to our planet, and one who said NSA was reading people's minds. It seems like NSA gets blamed for a lot it doesn't do, unless they really can do some of those bizarre things. NSA sued the developer of Pretty Good Privacy, an encryption tool, because they said it was exported encryption without a license required under the Arms Export Control Act[99]. Three years later, they dropped the suit. And, NSA and the Justice Department brought charges for espionage against Drake, the whistleblower. They eventually dropped this charge and reduced it to a misdemeanor. The suit limits damage and tampers down the heat, so it is always an option. "I'm sorry, we can't comment on on-going investigations" seems to be an acceptable excuse for anyone whether they are the one who brought the action, or the subject of it. Usually the threat is enough to get a negotiation going.

The threat of suit goes a long way. I got a briefing once from a person who was being watched very closely by a U.S. company because he claimed (and could prove) they used a trivial encryption scheme (easy to break) internal to one of their well-known products. [They couldn't follow him to this briefing since he was in a highly classified facility.] A few months before, he presented his case in a paper at a conference and a representative of the company sought him out. Most of the government people he worked with were already aware of the problem with working with this tool. It didn't protect information internally the way the vendor said it would. They told him that if he ever presented this in public, they would bring legal action against him. When he asked them, "For what?", the person said, "Because we can; we don't have to have a reason". He continued to do the briefing and deleted the name of the company. He said, "For months, they followed me around the country and had someone there, every time I spoke." They never realized the graphic in the background of his slide on the subject had a symbol easily recognizable as the company name.

The threat of a suit didn't deter him, but it would work for many of us who don't want that kind of distraction, when it is avoidable. What complicates our lives is the lack of marking of company trade secrets as secrets. When I worked at EDS, there was very little to see that said "Company Proprietary" but they were better than most other companies (with the possible exception of IBM) in putting something on a document that said it was protected. Some places never marked anything except formal slide shows, and most of the times, it was because the template was marked that way. EDS also had a pretty good non-disclosure agreement that kept people in line after they left the company. HP bought EDS, but didn't change the non-compete agreement and if you search on non compete agreements on the Internet, you can see why. EDS is mentioned more often than any other company because they have one of the best around. How much good it does them, is another matter.

What happened to the IT industry was a general cut back that had an effect on the whole sector of business. When the economy started to shrink people were being laid off. Those companies had agreements with their employees that said they not only wouldn't use secrets in another place, but they wouldn't go to a place that competed with the company we were coming from. Suddenly, a lot of people were looking for jobs and they were not supposed to be looking in places that competed with each other and they couldn't use the knowledge they got in one place to get a job somewhere else. Anyone who asked their lawyer was told that these agreements were enforceable, but might not be enforced. That isn't the type of guidance I look for from an attorney.

When people go without work for a little while, that kind of thing gets less clear, and less important. It can get ugly, if the company wants to enforce agreements that keep a person from being employed in a field where they worked their whole career, and all the companies were starting to get the idea that this was not going to work very well. All of us were respectful of EDS's agreement, until Mark Hurd left the company.

Mark Hurd was HP's CEO after HP bought EDS. He was going to work for one of HP's biggest competitors, Oracle. HP filed a civil lawsuit in California saying his move would endanger HP's trade secrets, but settled two weeks later, in a settlement that gave them part of Hurd's compensation package.[100] Mr. Hurd still sits at Oracle, years later. The shareholders sued HP (and lost) over the amount of compensation paid to Hurd when he left HP. Oracle sued HP in the same court. They are suing each other over various other things too, but the fun of it has sort of bottomed out.

The Non-disclosure Agreement

The government has more interesting ways to limit the exposure of National Security secrets. People outside of government are not very informed about procedures that were started in the Reagan Admin-istration to have any person who held a high-level clearance, submit to government censors anything they write for public consumption, before it is published. It can technically be anything I publish, or anything that Seal Team Six says to game or movie makers.

This whole process is tied up in National Security language that makes it sound like the government is using its knowledge of what is secret, and what is not, to make sure former government employees do not blab secrets to the world. On the whole, this sounds like a good thing, especially because they occasionally do blab them, and get caught.

Last year, there was a case where a person published a book with some Very Big Secrets in it and the government had to go around and get those books back [101]. The Army had already approved that book for public release, so they obviously didn't do a really good review of it. It may seem that "better late than never" is a good idea, but they must be kidding themselves because it is not possible, these days, to protect something that has already in a publisher's hands. The secret is now known by several people, who have no security clearance, and are scattered all over the world. There would be quite a few computers with this book in it, and it is nearly impossible to get all the copies back.

I read a couple of books about the military operations in Afghanistan and wondered, at the time, how such things can get into print when they tell all kinds of Very Big Secrets. They say when certain operations were done, who did them, and how they were carried out. They even talk about what other agencies and countries were doing. These are books that generally describe how well we are doing in some war. The Defense Departments seems perfectly willing to allow these books to be published, secrets or not, if they show how well the military is doing in some area of warfare. Once in awhile, they even tell us what the super-secret CIA has been doing in all kinds of places, but you will never hear that from the CIA. They know about Never Say Anything and they do a good job of following that rule. The rest of the government falls a little short.

The classic example of this is the way CIA handled the deaths in Khost, Afghanistan where several sources said they had lost 7 people when an agent blew himself up in their camp[102]. Just a quick look at the stories from that week will point out that it was not the CIA telling about what happened there. Everybody at CIA said "no comment" when asked about it, including the Director. Later, there was a report issued by CIA admitting that mistakes were made on several fronts, which is not exactly a secret. Press speculation created all kinds of examples of "what actually happened", but nobody will ever know what happened, because CIA keeps their mouths shut. So where, early on, do we get stories about the agents, the spy, the bombing, and all the rest?

The New York Times and Financial Times quoted "a U.S. official". In other articles, "some members of the Obama Administration" are quoted as saying the Times Square bomber was a similar intelligence failure [103].

A couple of others also quoted "former CIA officials" and MSNBC quoted "Western Intelligence Officials" which is really extending things a bit, since we are now talking about the possibility that the sources are not from the U.S.[104] They could be anyone, anywhere, though probably not China, Syria, Cuba or Iran. Anybody who has ever touched an intelligence service anywhere and who might know something, or be able to speculate on it, can talk about it even though we know that it is a Very Big Secret. These are the kinds of Very Big Secrets that need to be protected because people can get hurt when they aren't. People who leak these have forgotten that part.

This does not seem to keep a Marine from writing a book on the killing of Osama Bin Laden, and we have already heard that he did not get the government's permission to publish his book. This is an interesting case because the author was there when Bin Laden was killed, and knows what happened. "Instant best seller", everyone says. This is why the government wants a review before it is published. If there is information in that book that can get someone killed, or just give away some secrets, it is already in the hands of the publisher, who probably doesn't have a need for that kind of information, but loves to have it. The publisher might even blab it all over the place in pre-release book promotions. This has happened before, and the CIA has taken on anyone who ever published something like this, whether it was classified information or not. They haven't lost yet. The Defense Department doesn't seem to be motivated to follow their direction.

You might be surprised by what the Reagan Administration originally wanted to implement in order to control leaks. They originally proposed a Censorship Board where the person submitting the article could not hear testimony of the review and could be fined if the person disclosed classified information. The Administration backed off of the idea, but the Intelligence Community has not given up. The intent was described this way by one of the few people to have written about it, Frederick Whately:

"The Reagan administration proposes to remedy this deficiency and clearly contemplates either one large censorship board or several smaller boards contained within the various governmental units. One "trial balloon," put forward by Assistant Attorney General Richard K. Willard, proposed that penalties up to $5,000 plus an unlimited amount for damages be meted out to those who leak classified information. These penalties and/or damages would be determined by administrative officers, rather than judges. Moreover, such an officer would hold a closed hearing to which even the lawyer for the alleged "leaker" could not gain entry unless he had been cleared to receive classified information." [105]

Two years ago, the Senate Intelligence Bill (S719, Section 403) tried giving the Director of National Intelligence (DNI) the ability to withhold government pensions from people who disclose classified information. It never did pass, but just the introduction of it would give a person in government a second thought about giving away what somebody thought of as a secret. That can be good or bad, depending on whether it is a secret, and whether the government was given the opportunity to review it beforehand. This isn't as simple as it sounds.

What is worse than the actual reviews for pre-publication, is the use of censorship that this review gives those in government. It is an inconsistent and time-consuming exercise. Every person who gets access to Sensitive Compartmented Information signs an agreement. The agreement was made for every agency in the Federal government by the Department of Justice, so it would be enforceable everywhere. It says:

"I understand that the purpose of the review described in paragraph 4 is to give the United States a reasonable opportunity to determine whether the preparation submitted pursuant to paragraph 4 sets forth any SCI. I further understand that the Department or Agency to which I have made a submission will act upon it, coordinating within the Intelligence Community when appropriate, and make a response to me within a reasonable time, not to exceed 30 working days from date of receipt."

This sounds reasonable, but the practice of it doesn't work out quite the same. In a recent case, the FBI took nine years [106] because they didn't like some parts of a book. Nine years is longer than 30 days. I submitted a paper that was critical of the Army's handling of money in the cyber security program and it was in review for seven months. That is longer than 30 days.

Second, the censorship is not very consistent, because it is supposed to be a classification review i.e. looking for things that are classified National Security Information and the writer does not have access to the classification guidance. They call this "an issue" and they return a redacted version, which removes the text that is in dispute. This kind of thing worked well in the days before computers, which is when this whole process was invented. The government had the same kinds of problems with censorship that the World War II censors had with letters to wives and sweethearts. The letters would come back with blacked out parts that might tell an enemy where the person was or where they were going. Now, we have e-mail and telephone calls that do the same thing and have lost the capability of ever censoring anything, but it doesn't keep them from trying. This is the worst kind of censorship because it allows the government to cover up its mistakes and abuse, by doing nothing. They want the author to give up and go away.

The writer, like the WWII soldier in his tent in Northern Italy, gets no guidance until he submits something for review, and then, gets a redacted copy back. Redacted is the same as censored, except it is supposed to be looking at whether something is classified or not.

I have one example from the first chapters of this book that can give my readers an example of how this redaction looks when it comes back. I had two, but one of my redaction examples was redacted.

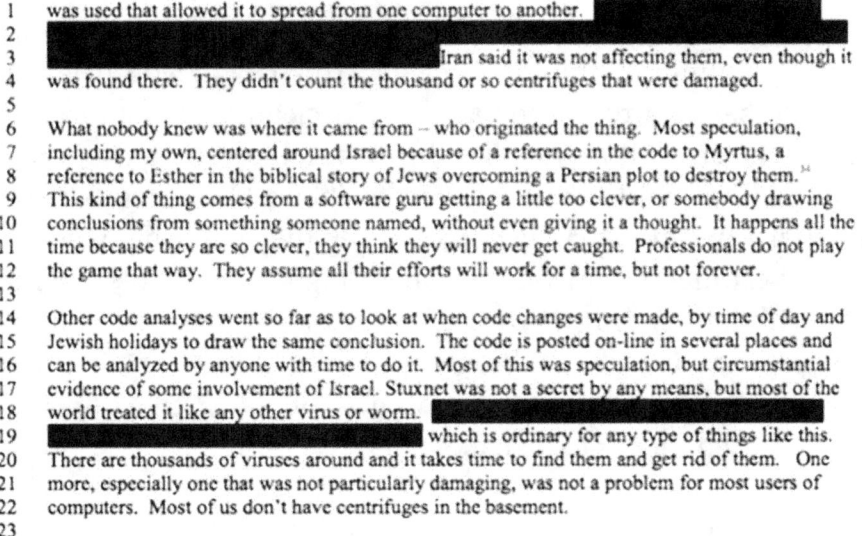

```
 1    was used that allowed it to spread from one computer to another. ████████████
 2    ███████████████████████████████████
 3    ████████████████████ Iran said it was not affecting them, even though it
 4    was found there. They didn't count the thousand or so centrifuges that were damaged.
 5
 6    What nobody knew was where it came from – who originated the thing. Most speculation,
 7    including my own, centered around Israel because of a reference in the code to Myrtus, a
 8    reference to Esther in the biblical story of Jews overcoming a Persian plot to destroy them.³⁴
 9    This kind of thing comes from a software guru getting a little too clever, or somebody drawing
10    conclusions from something someone named, without even giving it a thought. It happens all the
11    time because they are so clever, they think they will never get caught. Professionals do not play
12    the game that way. They assume all their efforts will work for a time, but not forever.
13
14    Other code analyses went so far as to look at when code changes were made, by time of day and
15    Jewish holidays to draw the same conclusion. The code is posted on-line in several places and
16    can be analyzed by anyone with time to do it. Most of this was speculation, but circumstantial
17    evidence of some involvement of Israel. Stuxnet was not a secret by any means, but most of the
18    world treated it like any other virus or worm. ████████████████████
19    ████████████████████ which is ordinary for any type of things like this.
20    There are thousands of viruses around and it takes time to find them and get rid of them. One
21    more, especially one that was not particularly damaging, was not a problem for most users of
22    computers. Most of us don't have centrifuges in the basement.
23
```

If a writer can footnote something, it is usually OK to say it. This makes writing a normal book, like you see in the supermarket, impossible, because every other paragraph or so, there will be a footnote. Donald Rumsfeld has 50 pages of notes in his book *Known and Unknown,* though others, like Michael Gordon and General Trainor, have done as well documenting their sources for the same reasons. But, they submitted their books for review, while other don't.

Third, the review process is not applied everywhere. Since I taught at a few universities, I knew some instructors who never submitted things for review, either their papers, their PhD theses, or their slide presentations for classrooms. None of them ever thought of these as "public release" since it was only being given to students. Students are the public, but the Federal government is going to stir up a hornet's nest to attempt to get anyone from colleges and universities to submit their papers to anyone for a classification review. They would rather ignore it. That isn't fair to those of us who do submit things.

Most writers never had security clearances, so they don't have to submit anything for review. This is why you have writers who have sources who had security clearances, but never had one themselves. It seems that they can tell a reporter and never tell anyone what they have given to them. How many bloggers are there out there that have everything they publish reviewed by the government? Can we say something on Facebook or Linkedin without sending it through a censor? Technically, it does have to be reviewed, but the application of the censorship process assumes the person being reviewed, submits it. They don't. The whole system needs to be fixed.

Polygraphs

About the first thing after the dust settled on the White House leaks in 2012, the Director of National Intelligence started calling for more polygraphs of government personnel and making some changes to the questions that were going to be asked. Polygraphs are "lie detector" tests which are supposed to say when a person is lying, but they don't do that very well. They can judge when certain questions are causing a physical reaction, maybe something like increased heart rate, that you can't even notice what is happening. This puts them in the same class of endeavor as Voodoo.

If a person believes in voodoo, they can be paralyzed by a spell or a little doll left on their seat at work. Aldrich Ames, at CIA, took polygraphs over and over but was still one of the biggest spies in U.S. history, so it is not something that will necessarily help them find one. Polygraphs were not admissible in court from 1923 until

1993[107], so we can get an idea of how sound a practice they were when I was taking them.

Polygraphs are supposed to be some kind of deterrent to blabbing secrets, but not many are convinced that it would work very well, or that we should be giving more of them, even if there was some cry for it. But, the second thing is, he was probably pointing a finger at the military, Executive and Legislative Branches of government, where polygraphs are not well thought of.

During the 9/11 debate on who knew what, when, there were leaks about intercepted phone conversations, saying NSA had intercepted calls from two suspects. The fact that they had been monitored was a secret. In the investigations of how that secret got out, the FBI was asked to investigate the Joint Congressional Committee on Intelligence and was asking if the members would like to submit to polygraphs. Alabama Sen. Richard Shelby, the ranking Senate Republican on the Joint Intelligence Committee, said "I don't know who among us would take a lie-detector test."[108] This kind of sets the stage for other Congressional people to say the same thing. Some White House people did too. Maybe they know something the rest of us don't, or they can get away with saying no. Both, probably.

Every year about two million people in industry and government are asked to take polygraph tests, but most military people are not. These can be anyone from a person like George Zimmerman who took two of them after he shot Treyvon Martin, or a guard who is trying to get employed to carry money around on a truck. About 300,000, or 7%, fail.[109] Nobody says whether a person fails, but they let them take another one to "validate" the first result. This may be because they are trying to be "fair" or it may be because they know they are not very reliable. Both of these things are true. The Voodoo priestess who puts the doll on a person's chair and finds the person out eating lunch instead of being hunched up in a ball in the corner, says, "Wait, let's try that again". The military has never favored polygraphs because they eliminate too many people and people are in short supply. It is possible to have two people doing the same job, and one gets to take polygraphs and the other does not have to. It is a ridiculous situation to have.

I can sympathize with anyone who fails, though we were always told we had to take the test again and not to say that we failed. If you fail, you can be working somewhere that doesn't require a security clearance until they figure out why. That may take a long time and that job is not going to be there when the whole process is over. That doesn't apply when taking a retest in a couple of weeks. If you are really worried about taking one, this two-week period can be a cooling off period or it can just make matters worse.

When you see a number like 300,000 a year that fail, there is not a direct correlation between the failing and not being hired or allowed to continue on a job. Everybody does the retesting thing because operators make mistakes, and there are always problems that can cause stress that have nothing to do with the readings an examiner is getting.

In 1993, the Supreme Court said the court can consider (1) whether the theory or technique on which the testimony is based is capable of being tested; (2) whether the technique has a known rate of error in its application; (3) whether the theory or technique has been subjected to peer review and publication; (4) the level of acceptance in the relevant scientific community of the theory or technique; and (5) the extent to which there are standards to determine the acceptable use of the technique. This opens things up a little, and gives science a chance to prove it can do something right. Of course it sort of makes me wonder what standard they were using before 1993, when I was taking them.

I admit to being baffled by pre-employment screening that is used by most businesses, but at least most of them stay away from polygraphs. In a way, these are similar to security clearances because they are really trying to answer the question of whether a person is trustworthy enough to work for that business and how much trust should they have. They might even try to discover if the person has the right kind of skills for the job they are going to be taking, but I haven't found that very often. In fact, pre-screening of employees is so tied up in privacy and other types of state legislation about what a company can ask or not ask, that it is almost worthless. The prescreening proves I worked before, but not how well, if I threatened my coworkers or anything else negative about me. The original purpose in doing it has long been cut off by laws that make no sense.

It has gotten so ridiculous that initial screening is mostly handled by Human Relations and, a few of those doing it are not located in the United States. I had the idea that being investigated by someone in the Philippines or Sri Lanka was not what a smart business would do, since so much of the information that goes into making that kind of decision is pretty sensitive. I don't know anyone in the Philippines and have no business there. I don't want them having my personal information, especially the types of things I have to tell a prospective employer. I told a company that recently, lost their consulting job, but felt better about the whole things afterwards.

Investigations by the Millions

Between the pre-employment screening done by industry and the investigations done for security clearances, every human being in the United States gets investigated at least once, and most of us, many times. What we have to believe is the results of an investigation of a person's past can predict what they will do in the future. Conversely, we can identify some things that will predict bad behavior, especially giving up secrets. Nobody knows whether this is true or not, but we have been doing it for a long time, so there must be some reason for it. Personally, I have my doubts about the whole idea.

Credit reporting, is used by almost any investigating activity. The reasoning for this is partly a belief that people in financial trouble are bad risks for keeping secrets and staying out of criminal behavior that might affect a company's bottom line. What they are really designed to do, is predict whether or not a person will pay back a debt that is owed. This has nothing to do with secret keeping, except indirectly. People in financial trouble may try to sell secrets or steal money. What we also have to believe is the inverse, that people who are not in financial trouble will not sell secrets or commit crimes. We know that neither of those is true.

We know that each of the large credit keeping agencies has a file on us, and anyone who has ever done a credit report on themselves, knows the three of them will not agree. They are never the same in each one of the credit agencies, and they take months to update when something has changed. When you asked investigators about the relationship between credit and crime they say, "it is just one indicator" and there are several that are used. That is a weak way of saying, "We aren't really sure about whether or not a person who has a bad credit history is a big risk, but we can tell you about it and let you decide."

This just means that they are not sure that any one indicator is important and judgment by an experienced adjudicator will work the variables. If there were only experienced adjudicators involved, I would have confidence in this system, but it isn't. We have managers, HR people, screening programs, consultants and all kinds of people doing this without any training at all.

Maybe decisions on information access have nothing to do with the investigation of backgrounds. The Federal government will issue an Interim Secret clearance with little more than a check to see if the person is a wanted felon. It only takes a couple of weeks to do, yet it takes over a year to get a clearance for the Really Big Secrets.

In this testimony before Congress[110], we see that every quarter the Office of Personnel Management is starting about 165,000 new investigations for people who are trying to get security clearances, and they claim they can process one of these in about 40 days. I laughed out loud at that one.

OPM PROGRESS FOR INITIAL CLEARANCE INVESTIGATIONS

			1st Qtr	2nd Qtr	3rd Qtr
	FY 2007	FY 2008	FY 2009	FY 2009	FY 2009
Total Completed	695,513	709,402	167,852	164,721	168,270
Average Time	115 Days	64 days	41 days	42 days	37 days

Time measured in calendar days

I'm not sure what planet these people were on when they made such a claim, but it takes longer than these figures suggest. GAO actually says it is closer to 60 days, and may be longer, depending on the agency involved[111]. When I worked for the Defense Investigative Service, we used to publish numbers like this too, saying that a security clearance investigation could be processed in 90 days or so, giving people the idea that they could actually get a clearance in that amount of time. They can get an interim clearance in that time, but it takes longer to get a final one. If a contractor wanted to get a new person a security clearance, I would allow 6 months. It may take longer, but 6 months is a good estimate. A high-level clearance takes about a year, or a good deal longer than 60 days.

In 2004, the US Code was changed to require the Federal government to do some fairly simple things to make it easier to get a security clearance. Remember, an investigation means you are eligible to have a clearance, but that doesn't mean you actually get one. This accounts for part of the time here between getting an investigation completed and getting a clearance, but not all of it.

The Code was changed to require a single agency to direct day-to-day oversight of investigations and adjudications of security clearances; implementing consistent policies and forms to fill out (I will skip the part about all the forms that are required but they are not easy to do); ensuring "reciprocal recognition" of access to classified information among the agencies of the United States Government. A rational person might think that changing the Code was a clue that they might have been having trouble with issuing security clearances. That would be an understatement.

Before the Code was changed, the government didn't have consistency, and still doesn't. That is what accounts for the rest of the time between getting an investigation and getting a clearance issued. Passing legislation does not deter places like the FBI, the Defense Intelligence Agency, Department of Energy, and Homeland Security that will not accept the clearance of another agency when they come to work there. At times, you cannot go from one part of the Defense Department to another without getting a new adjudication at the new place. It is worse for contractors who have to get adjudications done at all of these different places to do work there. Contractors sometimes have to get a new adjudication to go from one contract to another, in the same agency. So, are they trying to out adjudicate one another? Yes. Occasionally they point to this and say, "see I found something you didn't and this person was not suitable to be cleared". It might even be true, now and again, but not often enough to justify the expense. It does keep a number of adjudicators employed, and this is a good thing, especially with unemployment up the way it is.

There is also the business of polygraphs, and although the numbers are small, this keeps some people employed too. Some agencies do still require a polygraph and most of them will not accept one done by another agency, although there are exceptions.

All the investigations, re-investigations, and adjudications do not change very much since only about 1% do not actually get a clearance when it is said and done. A lot more than that give up waiting for one, and drop out of the system. They don't count in the 1%. This is statistics like the jobless rate in the country. We never know how many drop out and stop looking for jobs with security clearances. It seems that the things we do to prevent someone from getting a clearance don't relate very well to the ability of people to keep them.

Having a clearance does not help very much either, since it seems that people with them are still the ones that end up giving away secrets, either by accident or on purpose. What security clearances do well, is keep really bad people from getting access to secrets. That is much easier to do than all the hoopla would indicate. The elaborate procedures of "due process" in granting access to information are probably broken for a different reason. All it takes is one person, with a need to make a few hidden secrets public. Bloggers and "Administration officials" do this every day. We just can't keep a secret.

---

97 Tom Frijins, *Keeping Secrets*, Quality, Quantity and Consequences, 13 December 2004, http://dspace.ubvu.vu.nl/bitstream/handle/1871/9001/KeepingSecrets.pdf;jsessionid=6CCE8AA0F8D927D515D1B75F5DBE9797?sequence=1

98 Christie Nicholson, Keeping Secrets Weighs You Down, Literally, Scientific American, 29 April 2012, http://www.scientificamerican.com/podcast/episode.cfm?id=keeping-secrets-weighs-you-down-lit-12-04-29 This study says that people who kept important secrets felt more burdened by them than those who kept less important ones.

99   Russel D. Hoffman, An Interview with Phil Zimmerman, High Tech Today, 2 February 1996, http://www.animatedsoftware.com/hightech/philspgp.htm

100 EDS Settlement Orders, Order and Final Judgement Approving Proposed Settlement, 6 August 2008 http://www.kellersettlements.com/documents/EDS_Final-OrderSettlement080608.pdf

101 Catherine Herridge, Exclusive: Pentagon Attempts to Block Book on Afgan War, September 10, 2010 http://www.foxnews.com/politics/2010/09/09/military-intelligence-attempts-block-book-afghan-war/

102 Richard A. Oppel Jr., Mark Mazzetti and Souad Mekhennet, *Attacker in Afghanistan was a Double Agent* Published: January 4, 2010, http://www.nytimes.com/2010/01/05/world/asia/05cia.html

103 Dombey, Daniel, CIA admits errors led to Afghanistan attack, http://www.ft.com/cms/s/0/ac0408f4-dbe5-11df-af09-00144feabdc0.html and Windren, Robert and Engel, Richard, NBC News, http://www.msnbc.msn.com/id/34687312/ns/world_news-south_and_central_asia

104 Windren, Robert and Engel, page 2

105 Frederick W. Whately, Reagan, *National Security, and the First Amendment: Plugging Leaks by Shutting Off the Main,* 8 May, 1984, Copyright Cato Institute,(used by permission, Cato Institute)

106 Steven Aftergood, *Court Rebuffs FBI Censorship of Manuscript*, http://www.fas.org/blog/secrecy/2009/05/court_rebuffs_fbi_censorship.html

107 The Supreme Court replaced the Frye test, which said testing results weren't scientific enough, with a new one founded on Daubert v. Merrell Dow Pharmaceuticals, 509 U.S. 579, 113 S.Ct. 2786, 125 L.Ed.2d 468 (1993). http://www.sualaw.com/Appearances-rticles/The_Law_of_Polygraph_Evidence.pdf

108 Ed O'Keefe, Court *Rebuffs FBI Polygraphs*, ABC News, 2 August (no year given) http://abcnews.go.com/US/story?id=91404&page=1 - .T9dlWCtYvhM

109 American Civil Liberties Union, *Briefing Paper #4, Lie Detector Testing*, undated, http://www.lectlaw.com/files/emp28.htm

110 50 U.S.C. § 435b : US Code - Section 435B: Security Clearances

111 Executive Office of the President, The Security Clearance Oversight Group, Consistent with Title III, of the Terrorist Reform and Terrorism Prevention Act, 2004, published February 2007, http://www.whitehouse.gov/sites/default/files/omb/assets/omb/pubpress/2007/sc_report_to_congress.pdf

CHAPTER 10

Losing Secrets by the Truckload

When we put all the secrets we have in computers, they become harder to keep, but we keep all of them in computers. This sounds like irony. As a concession to my friends in computer security where I earned my living for 40 years, I would add that it has little to do with the ability of computers to be secure repositories for data. We can make them secure; we just don't and that tells us something important to the keeping of secrets. We sometimes say that protecting secrets is important, but we don't act like it. This is especially true when it comes to protection of information in computer networks.

Years ago, I found a way to get into IBM computers that was pretty interesting and hard to detect. I wrote to IBM about it, rather than just take their data. Not everybody is like that. Robert Courtney, IBM's Security Director (at that time) wrote back a simple truth about secrets. He said, "Yes, what you are proposing will work, but it is not as important as you might think. We lose more information by accident than we lose on purpose." What he was saying was intentionally stealing information doesn't come close to matching what we do by accident. I'm not sure that is still true, but nobody keeps score on this either.

It is certainly worth thinking more about, because what is intentional, and what is accidental, is not as clear as it used to be. We certainly know that there are many, many problems with our electronic devices and most of them are accidents, if you call a programming error an accident. I don't, but I may be in the minority among developers.

Every few weeks, we hear about a new cell phone vulnerability that needs attention. The "we" here is the computer security community, not the people who lease cell phones. A recent report for Android phones says there were forty-one different ones, some that allowed hackers access to personal data stored on the phone that were newly discovered. [112] The nature of a problem like this is that it can be a screen that comes up blank because the text color is white on a white background, or it can be something that causes the phone to fail in some rare set of circumstances, and will take a long time to discover. It might even be a really serious problem that lets hackers have access to personal data on the phone, like my bank password. I don't want that one to go on for a month, but I don't get a say in this. Only Verizon and the vendor have a say.

The second part of this is we never know if it is an accident, or it was done on purpose. You may remember that Google figured out how to get around the feature of the Apple browser that allows an Apple user to keep search information from Google. Google did a "work-around" and got the information anyway. Apple didn't like that very much and the Federal Trade Commission told Google to stop doing it.[113] Google countered by making their Chrome browser for Apple systems. This is a game of big companies, all with something to gain, but we never know what that might be. To users, it is not a game we want to play. A Russian or Chinese hacker may be doing this on purpose by planting something in the designer's software that he keeps at home. We never know who did what, or why.

The truth of the matter is the cell phone I carry is not mine. It belongs to Verizon and Verizon does not make cell phones; it just leases them to people like me. Verizon is pretty responsive to security matters, but they don't make the operating systems of phones, the applications that run on them, nor even sometimes, the software that runs the cell towers they use to get my signal to their big pipes. By the time they find out there is a problem with something or another, they have to go to a vendor that does.

The vendor can say to Verizon, "We are really sorry about that and we will put together a team and correct that problem in a couple of weeks." Verizon might not think the particular thing should wait for a couple of weeks that-generally-stretches-to-a-month, but they are not in a position to get something done much faster. The vendor can say, "That doesn't look like a problem with our software; that seems to be a problem with the Ajax Corporation software, so we are not fixing anything. These things take longer until somebody figures out who is really the culprit here. In the meantime, we are exposed to this type of risk for various amounts of time, and it is the vendors who decided how long that is. There are more of these risks than just ones that are made by software.

In 2010, NASA managed to sell some surplus computers that had secrets on them, and this has happened almost every year since the 80's when one of our government agencies sold government secret computers to a junk dealer, in Kentucky, who would not sell them back. I can't begin to tell you the number of laptops people in the government and commercial business lose every year, and I doubt that they will say. But, this is probably why the Chinese buy our paper and metal trash, about $8 billion of it[114]. There are enough things found in it, to make getting rid of the trash worthwhile.

Every once in awhile somebody has to offer a few thousand people identify theft protection because their names and various types of personal data were lost on a laptop somewhere. The value of that information to the vendor who lost it is about $50-100, the cost to them of having identify theft protection put up for each of the people who request it. If it is on a disk in the trash that China got, they probably won't tell us they have it. But, how the vendor looks at it is not the same to me. I have to watch my credit cards, lines of credit, and bank accounts very closely for the next year. The coverage they buy for me is so slow in recording them that the thief will be off and running with my money by the time they figure out it is gone. They say, "we will cover that loss for you" and I say "that isn't good enough" because it will damage my credit rating for a long time after they have paid for the loss. My time and reputation isn't worth anything to them.

Twelve million Americans have their identities stolen every year and the number goes up 10% or more, every year., a factor the Wall Street Journal partially attributes to the increasing use of mobile devices,[115] like the Verizon phone I have. People never seem to learn to keep track of them. Besides that, they lose smartphones, cell phones, portable disk drives, copy machines, cameras, briefcases and more. When we were losing pieces of paper, there was not much lost in each one of these incidents, but not anymore. Some copy machines have terabyte drives and have personal and proprietary data on them. If I lose my own Blackberry, it is my fault, but if someone leaves my personnel data on the hard drive of a copy machine, they don't know who did it and I won't know how those thieves got my credit card number. I have nobody to appeal to. We don't even know if someone did it on purpose, unless it is something big enough that we can see it.

The talking point in Washington Committee hearings has been China, which seems to have found out it is easier to steal technology than to develop it. Before them, the Russians were onto this concept for at least 10 years and stole everything they could get their electronic hands on. Now, they seem to have combined their efforts in China, which offers protection against prosecution as long as target isn't Chinese. The Chinese control their Internet better than any other country. This cozy arrangement is not doing us any good, but nobody can do very much about it. It is part of their national strategy.

Starting in November of 2010, several systems were hacked by someone who established over 300 control systems, almost all around Beijing. What made this different was the attackers were going after RSA, famous for its ability to do encryption. RSA says they were never told about where the attacks were coming from, and the loss of data from them was not tied to any losses by their customers. A SANS report[116] says somebody emulated enough information in an RSA token to get into Lockheed, and Lockheed says they got in using a token, without saying who's token it was. [117]

During the next few months, several other major companies were hacked in the same way, using almost exactly the same types of methods. [118] There is the IRS, USAA which primarily handles insurance and banking for military people, several locations of COMCAST and Computer Sciences Corporation, a few locations of IBM, the US Cert, which handles investigations into computer incidents at the Federal level, the Defense Department Network Information Center, Facebook, Fannie May, Freddie Mac (just so we have most of those housing loans covered), Kaiser Foundation Health Care System, McAfee Inc - the virus people, Motorola, Wells Fargo Bank (and Wachovia, now owned by Wells Fargo), MIT, University of Nebraska-Lincoln, University of Pittsburg, VMWare, the World Bank, and almost every telecommunications company of any size, anywhere in the world. That last one included all the major telecoms in China, so, they are hacking their own telecoms. If a group is going after everything, they are not a bunch of kids working out of a back room in a run-down office complex.

There were 760 companies in all, and 20% of the Fortune 100, but nobody is saying these people have stopped hacking. They are still at it. It would also be nice to know how much information was really lost. How many hard drives were involved; how many storage systems? how many users? Saying it was 20% of the Fortune 100 doesn't really tell a person what kind of damage came from it. It is like saying you lost a laptop, or 100 laptops. We can say, for sure, that we lost a boatload of data to China, but that isn't very satisfying to know. I want to know if the measure is Petabytes or Exobytes, then try to make sense of a number that big. I know that when I see a Chinese fighter that looks a lot like a Euro Fighter, but I would be hard pressed to say that it means the Chinese stole the designs from the company that makes it. We would never know if they just copied it, or stole the exact manufacturing details. These days, when a hacker steals electronic designs, he also steals the ability to machine the parts on certain types of computer-aided equipment. It becomes easier to build.

When computers were young they had small drives that could barely hold enough to make them worth the $2000 that I paid for my first one in 1982. Now for the same amount, I get a 500 gigabit drive and enough memory to never use it all (although I said that about the one I bought in 1982, and was wrong). Some of the space missions downloaded gigabit platters every day and that was at the beginning of space flight, so they could have filled up my 500 gigabit drive twice in the same day. We now talk about military missions where the storage requirements run into petabytes every day. That is a number that is really hard to imagine. There is a cute visualization summary of what a petabyte is at http://mozy.com/blog/misc/how-much-is-a-petabyte/. In video terms, it is about 13 years of HD-TV. I can't imagine HD TV having 13 years of watchable material, but the military is not in the entertainment business. When someone steals a petabyte of data, they are stealing more than we want to think about. It takes awhile to download that much data, and you would hope someone would notice.

Wired magazine published a story, June 2010, that shows some instant message exchanges between Bradley Manning, the supposed WIKILEAKS source and former hacker Adrian Lamo who turned him in[119]. In it, Manning talks about using a music CD to copy information. Most of these hold about almost 5 gigabits. If I lose one of those, I can lose 120 feet of books lined up beside one another. That is the same distance as it takes my car to stop from 60 miles per hour when that deer walks out onto the road. If that computer has a 500 gigabit drive on it, we lose enough to make an impression on the folks at WIKILEAKS or any of the news agencies. You will notice the government never says how much information they lost; they just say they lost a laptop.

Imagine what happens when a hacker gets into an office of a major company and gets access to 50 or 60 of those disks and some bigger storage systems. The government certainly knew how many companies got hit, but I didn't get notices from everyone that lost information. The Wall Street Journal and USAA Insurance Company were exceptions that reported it within a couple of weeks of the loss occurring. I didn't find out about the rest of them until I started doing research on the number and extent of Chinese hacking incidents. How much information did the Chinese really get? The average person will never find out, because nobody in government will tell us, but more importantly, they probably don't know.

There is one report that sheds a little light on this subject and it is called *APT1, Exposing One of China's Espionage Units*[120], by Mandiant Corporation, a small company that does Internet threat detection, tracing the threats back to their electronic hosts.[121] Mandiant helped the New York Times find out they were hacked by China, particularly a group of PLA soldiers operating from an address they had seen before.

I'm usually skeptical of this type of claim because I watched hackers operate for many years and where they are good, they do not get caught, especially where they are operated by a government. Governments use well-funded and well-trained people to do this kind of work and they know what they are doing. A spokesman for the

Chinese Academy of Sciences Institute and Computing Technology (ASICT) said Chinese hackers "were not smart enough to steal data from U.S. businesses", so we would have to wonder where those hackers got their skills. This novel thought process indicates the ASICT has both a slanted view of the hacker world in China, and a good sense of humor. However, on those rare times when they can be monitored for a long period of time, which Mandiant seems to have done, there are a lot of things that can be learned about their operations. They claim to have been following this one group since 2006.

Watching hackers over time is hard to do but has great benefits. The problem is whether or not the operation can afford the losses of information while the hackers are being followed. From 1998-2000 we followed one small group of six people and they were able to get into almost every network they tried because they were persistent and had quite a bit of time on their hands. We were interested in how they did it, but conflicted over how much of it had to be reported to those being attacked. We saw them use brute-force attacks on password files, store their information on another computer that was hacked for that purpose, change locations of their attacks so they appeared to come from other countries, and collect tools they used to build software. They tested their software and improved it before applying it to systems they were attacking. Some attacks were short and they never went back to those places, and some lasted for over a year. They were not very advanced in their techniques at first, but they got better as time went on. Eventually, they came up with a way send a large number of requests to a website so that it would become overwhelmed or slow down the service and they were doing these attacks from other computers, not their own. Our bosses felt like this too big to allow and went to law enforcement to shut them down. Keeping the hacker tracking secret is difficult to do.

In six years, as Mandiant found, hackers can do more damage than anyone could imagine, especially if they are organized and have money behind them. In one instance, they observed the Army unit stealing 6.5 Terabytes from a single organization over a 10-month period (page 25). That isn't very much information but the quality might have been good. I have been trying to fill up a 1 Terabyte disk for over a year, but I'm not out stealing it from other people. That would make things go faster.

With the size of disks getting to be 2 Terabytes on a laptop, we can soon see the amount of data lost in this organization easily fitting on a single hard disk. Now, even when they get access to 141 these disks, they don't have very much information – in data processing terms, anyway.

In another case, they observed a penetration that lasted two and a half years and was reading the e-mail of the President and General Counsel of the company. During that time, the Chinese negotiated a much lower ("double-digit") unit price on goods purchased from the company. This indicates they are not only stealing, but plowing it back into the economic war they are fighting with us. They were stealing information from multiple companies, world-wide but mostly in the U.S., and from different sectors of the economy:

Information Technology	Transportation	High-Tech Electronics
Financial Services	Navigation	Legal Services
Engineering Services	Media/Advertising	Food and Agriculture
Satellites and Telecoms	Chemicals	Energy
International Organizations	Scientific Research	Public Administration
Construction and Manufacturing	Aerospace	Education
Healthcare		Metals and Mining

(*APT1*, pages 23-24)

163

In all, they observed hacking at 141 different targets, in 15 countries. On average, after penetration of a system, they stayed inside the network for over a year. They had a large infrastructure to support this kind of theft, with 109 servers in the U.S. and various single-digit numbers in 12 other countries, 13, if you want to count China. They worked out of a building that was 130,000 square feet and had hundreds of employees. They didn't need 109 servers if the only information they were gathering came from those 141 systems Mandiant was seeing.

Keep in mind, Mandiant is only reporting on one active hacking organization. They recognize there may be some they missed. Contrast that with the six people we were following.

A similar type of hacking is taking place in China itself. One-forth of U.S. companies in China claim they have had trade secrets stolen through their Chinese operations.[122] It is easier for China to hack systems in China since they use networks operated there and linked to government activities. They are already in subsidiaries of companies and can hack back to their corporate headquarters without exposing themselves to much risk. That applies equally to many other countries that monitor corporate networks, and is not unique to China. But what makes this more exasperating for the people being affected is the inability of Chinese courts to enforce intellectual property rights and technology control requirements. Once the data is stolen, it can be –and is- used to set up competing companies, competing products, and manipulate bids.

The volume of data involved is important because we are getting into something called *big data,* the storage of vast amounts of information in clouds, using specialized software that structures and retrieves it, almost as easily as a personal computer does the same thing. The problem with big data lies in the ability to hack big quantities if we have an enterprising group that knows much of anything about how to get into somebody else's computer system. U.S. companies increasingly do not trust China as a partner in the cloud.[123] Only 10% of U.S. companies would consider using a cloud environment that was based in China and 40% of them are concerned about the rising threat of data theft by China. The unfortunate part is that no vendor will admit to having a cloud environment with Chinese partner, so it is going to be difficult to discover which ones actually do.

This affects our national security because it allows the Chinese to unfairly compete with us, and it is more than just subsidizing solar panels that end up in U.S. markets. Every single detail of this is involved in both the government and business ability to do good computer security. They are terrible at it; they ignore the consequences, and the Chinese are quick to seize the advantage.

Our Secrets in Government Computers

In the world of classified information, the idea that a person could have a TOP SECRET clearance and get access to all levels of secrets was over-simplified. There was SCI that not everyone was allowed to see just because they were cleared to that level. There were thousands of these little places. There were some Special Access Programs that only certain people with SCI Access could see. So not only did you have to figure out how to give access to people who were cleared, but they also had to be authorized into the compartment. There were so many variables to this that it was not easy to map them out, but that is what they were doing; then, they would figure out what had to be done to implement these through security mechanisms at every level of the network. It was complicated and they had no idea how it could be done.

Over the years, the Defense Department spent more money than I can count, doing this over and over, trying to get it right. They put PCMCIA slots on their computers so we could add little black boxes to encrypt everything so it couldn't be hacked by anyone. We had slots on computers, for years, waiting for the cards to be built, but no cards. We had specialized servers and all kinds of routers and things that just made a person feel warm and comfortable to have them right there on desks. I don't know how much all of that cost, but it was more than I ever made in my career and it wasn't worth a nickel to anyone. Nothing we tried worked very well, except cutting our networks off from the Internet. That works pretty well, but nobody could look at outside e-mail, check a website, or their on-line shopping so it doesn't go over well with the users. We were hoping something would come of it and bring security to the Net before we all got old, but it hasn't happened yet.

Nobody can do it now, either. After forty years of building the Internet children of ARPANET, we can't do the security that was envisioned at the time. The government, especially the Defense Department, somehow never got it right. At some point we need to say, "that is not possible to do, so let's look at the problem another way".

It gets harder to do because we have not stopped making new categories of secrets, and we still can't do security of the ones we had before. Only now, all our secrets are in those networks and we almost never write them down on paper the way we used to. We do banking on line, social networking, pay for cups of coffee, and link to everyone on e-mail. We have endless exchanges of secrets of various kinds. Now we have all the Really Big Secrets, and the smaller ones, all mixed in together. Protecting those secrets is something we do not do very well.

It is certainly not a technical problem. We know how to build very secure networks. For those in the government and commercial sectors where secrets are important, like the CIA, the Federal Reserve, and the large credit card processing systems, protecting secrets is part of their culture. They work at it. They live it. But the vast majority of government and business don't. There is really no difference between them. Both are equally bad at it.

When we have something going on for such a long time, and we speak of it as if it were a new problem, there is something fundamentally wrong with the way we are engaging how we address it. This is not about technology, or ease of use; it is about the ability of people in IT to do security of their information systems. They do not do very well at it; the problem goes deep in both government and the commercial sector; and there will not be any improvement in information systems security until there are fundamental changes in the way we view it and perform it. It is not a technical problem.

Stealing Information is Not New

Having the CIO's e-mail read by a hacker in Russia, especially when that person can say with impunity, "Yes, I know you know, but you can't do anything about it" is very uncomfortable for the people sitting in the room. There are really two sides to this problem: (1) the ability of thieves to get into systems, and (2) the ability of almost anyone to get things out, without anyone knowing they did it. Neither one is too difficult, but advances in stealing will follow behind technology for time before they catch up. Examples from physical security are easy to follow.

A good thief is quick and can undo a lock in a few seconds, making us wonder why we bought those locks to begin with. A car thief can steal or strip a car in what seems like seconds in spite of an industry that works on keeping them from doing it. Even people who stole a backhoe and tried to crack open an ATM at one of our local banks, last week, was trying to show initiation in the way they stole money. Computer thieves are better, smarter, and much more capable than anyone who makes a living stealing things from physically secure places. They have to be.

Global networks are not simple and hackers have to be able to get around in them. They can operate from other countries which favor their legal status, or they can switch identities quickly to becomes someone else. They steal, and there is no ATM lying on the sidewalk outside to tip people off. We seem to believe the Chinese are stealing everything from us, when it may not only be the Chinese. Groups of people may be stealing from us, but this only makes China guilty of stealing relatively more information, not innocent. My first experience with foreign hackers was with Russia, the middle 1980's. Nobody was talking about the Chinese then.

In the 1990s some clever people teamed with us in Ballistic Missile Defense to track hackers and find out what they were developing. We were not looking at the threats of today, but ones that were new or would develop into something bad in the future. We assumed missile defense would not be viable for another 10 years and we had to see the threats 10 years out.

In 1998, there was a great deal of publicity about Moonlight Maze, Russian hackers in US systems, which Vernon Loeb, Washington Post Staff Writer reported this way: [124]

> "A series of sophisticated attempts to break into Pentagon computers has continued for more than three years, and an extensive investigation has produced "disturbingly few clues" about who is responsible, according to a member of the National Security Agency's advisory board.
>
> The NSA consultant, James Adams, says U.S. diplomats lodged a formal protest with the Russian government last year after investigators determined that the cyber attacks, which they code-named "Moonlight Maze," appear to have

originated from seven Russian Internet addresses. But Russian officials replied that the telephone numbers associated with the sites were inactive and denied any prior knowledge of the attacks, according to Adams.'

"Meanwhile, the assault has continued unabated," Adams wrote in this month's Foreign Affairs magazine, published by the Council on Foreign Relations. "The hackers have built 'back doors' through which they can re-enter the infiltrated systems at will and steal further data; they have also left behind tools that reroute specific network traffic through Russia."

Moonlight Maze[125] popped up in the press several times between 1999 and 2000 partly because the Senate was holding hearings in the Governmental Affairs Committee to try to foster legislation that would help prevent or deter hacking in the U.S. Moonlight Maze had detected Russian hackers making extensive inroads into NASA, The Army Corps of Engineers, several areas of the Pentagon and our military. That had been going on for two years when it was detected. The GAO said there were 1300 attacks against Army, Navy and Air Force systems, 700 of which were "serious", leaving us to our imaginations for a definition of the term. If that sounds familiar, it should, because Congress is doing the same thing again this year for about the same reasons. The main change is in who is being blamed for the hacking going on. That shift publically took place around 2005 with Titan Rain.[126]

Here too, hackers were getting into computer systems in the Defense Department, State, Energy, Homeland Security and other Federal agencies and it had been going on for at least two years when detected. The Post article says "The number of attempted intrusions from all sources identified by the Pentagon last year totaled about 79,000, defense officials said, up from about 54,000 in 2003. Of those, hackers succeeded in gaining access to a Defense

Department computer in about 1,300 cases. The vast majority of these instances involved what a Defense spokesman called "low risk" computers. We are starting to see a pattern here.

I got to see a very small part of what we were dealing with when a hacker got into a military base. Everyone thought it was the Russians because it looked like the attacks they had been running in the United States. We were right in the middle of Moonlight Maze and everyone was keen to launch a strike against the enemy.

The military base that had been hacked seemed to be having trouble getting the hacker out of the systems, even after they had identified how he had gotten in. Some of our experts were advising them and the good guys were getting frustrated. Every time they got him out of the network, within a couple of days, he was back in. They assumed there had to be some kind of "back door" or Trojan horse planted in the network that was allowing him to return. They spent many hours looking for their methods, but nothing seemed to work. The military unit gave up and asked for help, so the Defense Information Systems Agency sent some people up there to analyze the attack. It took them weeks to stop the attacks and months of post-attack work to clean up the entire site. Since that incident, the military group there has become top experts in hacking, but none of us looked like experts when it was over.

It turned out a 14-year old in the U.K. had been doing this work and he had learned from what he was seeing on the Internet about how the Russians had been doing their attacks, collecting some of their tools and trying them out. He was only one person, using what he learned. This age group has time for most anything they set their minds to, and this fellow chose getting into other computer systems and staying there. Keep in mind that this was 25 years ago and hacking has advanced quite a bit since then. Our experts now call it the Advanced Persistent Threat, but that is what it was back then too. Once people get into a network, it is very hard to get them out. When they get in at multiple locations, it is nearly impossible.

I made an observation back then that the only safe systems we saw were banking networks, but that only refers to the financial transaction side of banking. The Chinese and Russian gangs have hacked major banks and siphoned off all kinds of records used to take money from people who were not even aware they were being hit. They attack the parts of the system that store information about clients and accounts. They use that information to help them get use of an otherwise secure network of financial transactions. They hit insurance companies for the same reason. Electronic banking, and financial transactions used to be safe. Not so much anymore. This kind of thing undermines our National Security by eroding confidence in our ability to do secure money transfers between our major financial institutions.

In 1994, Russian student Vladimir Levin, and his gang hack into Citibank and steal more than $10 million, at the time the biggest computer heist ever. Levin and his accomplices used stolen access codes and passwords to transfer funds across the United States, Europe, and Israel. Months after he's discovered, he's arrested by Interpol and extradited to the U.S. to stand trial, where he made a plea bargain.[127] Last year, someone did better than Levin and was equally clever at how they did it. They managed to get debit card limits raised and went around New York, and various other places, sucking money out of ATMs where they could get access.

People are starting to get the idea that banks were not as safe as they once thought.

A few years after Levin, the leadership of the Defense Department said this type of attack showed the weaknesses in the defense of our computer networks, but they surely did not need this type of incident to prove the point, nor ten years to figure it out.

"As a result of these analyses, we have identified information security as a government-wide high-risk issue in reports to the Congress since 1997—most recently in January 2001. These weaknesses continue as indicated by our most recent analyses for these 24 large federal agencies that considered the results of inspector general (IG) and GAO audit reports published from July 2000 through September 2001, including the results of the IGs' independent evaluations of these agencies' information security programs performed as required by GISRA [*The Government Information Security Reform Act* requires government offices to have procedures and programmatics to make their systems secure]. These analyses showed significant information security weaknesses in all major areas of the agencies' general controls, that is, the policies, procedures, and technical controls that apply to all or a large segment of an entity's information systems and help ensure their proper operation."

From 1998 to the present, our government has demonstrated, over and over, that computers are not safe places to keep secrets. We should start thinking about what needs to be done to make them more safe than they are. Why didn't we do that 20 years ago, when these types of attacks started to come up? First, because it costs money and builders of computers would rather not spend that kind of money to make systems safe. They act like they believe the secrets are not that important. Secondly, because people always believe that they are protecting information better than they actually are, even with contrary evidence staring them in the face. They don't want to work at finding out how bad their security really is. At the highest levels of government, this is a complicated thing.

Moonlight Maze, a demonstration that Russia was hacking U.S. sites, and almost 10 years later, Titan Rain, a similar set of cases showing Chinese are doing the same thing, are just two of the reasons the money was given to these agencies, and there seems to be no end to take weaknesses in our defensive posture and milk them for whatever the Congress is willing to spend on it. They are doing it repeatedly and nobody is watching where the money goes or why we have to spend more each time to get the same result.

It is not an anomaly in government or business. This is kind of the same as the store owner who see snow piling up outside on his sidewalk but can't get the time to clear a path for the customers. If one of them falls, he gets sued, but he will take the chance for now. They have other priorities and security of their computer systems is not one of them.

There were a succession of Inspector General reports written about different Agencies, including Defense, Justice, FBI, EPA, State and the Veterans Administration that pointed to persistent and deep problems with the way information systems security was being done. Most of them are repeat offenders, and continue to be poor, even now:

> "Since September 1996, we have reported that poor information security is a widespread federal problem with potentially devastating consequences. Although agencies have taken steps to redesign and strengthen their information system security programs, our analyses of information security at major federal agencies have shown that federal systems were not being adequately protected from computer-based threats, even though these systems process, store, and transmit enormous amounts of sensitive data and are indispensable to many federal agency operations. In addition, in both 1998 and 2000, we analyzed audit results for 24 of the largest

federal agencies and found that all 24 had significant information security weaknesses.

As a result of these analyses, we have identified information security as a government-wide high-risk issue in reports to the Congress since 1997—most recently in January 2001. These weaknesses continue as indicated by our most recent analyses for these 24 large federal agencies that considered the results of inspector general (IG) and GAO audit reports published from July 2000 through September 2001, including the results of the IGs' independent evaluations of these agencies' information security programs performed as required by GISRA.7 These analyses showed significant information security weaknesses in all major areas of the agencies' general controls, that is, the policies, procedures, and technical controls that apply to all or a large segment of an entity's information systems and help ensure their proper operation."

> Critical Infrastructure Protection: Significant Homeland Security Challenges Need to Be Addressed July 09, 2002.

We have known about the weaknesses for the past 25 years. I certainly don't want somebody running this show to be telling me what I need to do about computer security. We have no crisis that is any different now than it was when it was first identified, and we don't understand the problems any better than we did then. We have a foundational business model that says we have control over the computer systems we own, and we can direct how they are secured, but in fact, we have no control over the software, the circuits that handle the data, leased equipment or outsourced services. Now, we are going to put all of these services in clouds and make it even harder to do. We have to focus on the goal of protecting our national networks from our enemies. Congress cannot even agree on simple things that need to be done to protect our national networks. Getting anything through Congress is proving impossible.

112 Sascha Fahl, Marian Harbach, Thomas Muders, Matthew Smith, Lars Baumgärtner, Bernd Freisleben, *Why Eve and Mallory Love Android: An Analysis of Android SSL (In)Security,* University of Hanover, copy write CCS'12, October 16–18, 2012, Raleigh, North Carolina, USA. http://www2.dcsec.uni-hannover.de/files/android/p50-fahl.pdf

113 Sara Forden, Google Said to Face Fine by U.S. over Apple Safari Breach, 9 August 2012, Bloomberg Technology, http://www.bloomberg.com/news/2012-08-09/google-said-to-face-fine-by-u-s-over-apple-safari-breach.html

114 Clyde Prestowitz, *America Needs a New Globalization Game,* Huffington Post 29 April 2012, online, accessed 11/05.2012, http://www.huffingtonpost.com/clyde-prestowitz/america-needs-a-new-globa_b_557131.html

115 Jennifer Waters, *Why ID Thieves Love Social Media,* Wall Street Journal, 25 March 2012 http://online.wsj.com/article/SB10001424052702304636404577293851428596744.html

116 Johannes Ullrich, *Lockheed Martin and RSA Tokens,* 30 May 2011 https://isc.sans.edu/diary/Lockheed+Martin+and+RSA+Tokens/10939

117 Christopher Drew, Stolen Data is Tracked to Hacking at Lockheed, New York Times, 3 June, 2011, http://www.nytimes.com/2011/06/04/technology/04security.html?_r=0

118 Krebs on Security, Who Else was Hit by the RSA Attackers, http://krebsonsecurity.com/2011/10/who-else-was-hit-by-the-rsa-attackers/

119 Kevin Poulsen and Kim Zetter, *I Can't Believe What I'm Confessing to You': The Wikileaks Chats,* Wired, June 10, 2010, http://www.wired.com/threatlevel/2010/06/wikileaks-chat/

120 http://intelreport.mandiant.com/?gclid=CK7Qssi09bYCFdJQOgodeWkAhw

121 Neal Underleider, *Hacked? Mandiant's Cyberattack Detectives want to know all about it,* FastCompany, 3 April 2013. http://www.fastcompany.com/3007761/code-war/hacked-mandiants-cyberattack-detectives-want-know-all-about-it

122 Jamil Anderlini, *Quarter of US groups in China claim to be cyber attack victims,* Financial Times, 30-31 March 2013

123 Carlos Tejada, *Many U.S. Companies in China Site Data Theft,* Wall Street Journal, Updated version 29 March 2013

124 [3.] Washington Post, Monday, May 7, 2001; Page A02

125 Elinor Abreu, *Cyber Attacks Reveal Cracks in U.S. Defense,* PCWorld, 9 May 2001

126 Bradley Graham, *Hackers Attack Via Chinese Web Sites,* Washington Post, 25 August 2005

127 Jessica Ramirez, *Educating Elite Hackers,* The Daily Beast, Mar 10, 2010

CHAPTER 11

The Value of a Lost Secret

The Chinese and Russians are focusing on computer systems that have so much information in them that they must have trouble sorting through all they have stolen. Doing this type of analysis is resource intensive and time-consuming, but nobody is feeling sorry for them. They must be finding out that there is a lot of trash in the folders of some of those users and it is just taking up space.

Our biggest mistake in managing information is in treating it all the same, when any analysts of information know it isn't. Some things are worth more than others, but we don't have a good way to say which ones are the most important. Our enemies take it all, and figure that part out later.

The biggest problem with information is how much of it we have. We know, for example, that the Stuxnet worm was interesting to the world long before the White House told us it was the U.S. developing it. The existence of the worm is not a secret, until we put it together with the place of origin. It does not take much more information than that simple fact to make a lot of other things in our databases make sense. The more information we accumulate, the more potential associations we can make. The information we keep, in the world, is doubling every year.

Businesses and government collect information they know they will probably never need, but they aren't sure about what they might need, so they keep what they can get. They are just never sure of what might be of value. They keep it around because, someday, it might make sense. I might get an employee who is a really good business analyst, who sees something in the mining of data that gives our company new insight about what our competitors are doing. We may use that to plot a new course on where the company is going. Intelligence services wait for something to help them out in making sense of all of their data, but only a small fraction of our government or business is in the intelligence business. Everyone keeps everything, whether they really need it or not, and that creates an opportunity to lose it, without really knowing it is gone.

When I was growing up in the security field, I was always taught – and later repeated to my own students – that information could be categorized into variants that showed their value. About 10 % of all information was really important; about 20% more was worth protecting but not as valuable, and the rest was fodder of some sort. I have no idea where these percentages came from, or whether those numbers were accurate. They just seemed right. That is a hard thing for me to admit, even now.

Certainly, in some places I have worked, there was very little that was not a Really Big secret, but outside of the Intelligence circles, there are not many places like that. The idea, at least through the history of computing, has been that we had some really big secrets that could be separated out and we could devote more energy and resources to protecting those than we did protecting the other 70%. Something has happened to change that idea, but it was not the simple fact that there was no real basis for those numbers.

My Social Security Number is a commodity to be traded by thieves, and my credit card numbers have all been stolen at least once, so I am starting to get the idea that those Top Secret things were not the most important secrets in the hands of the people

I deal with. Neither one of those show up in the list of National Interests, but they are of equal importance to anyone who has had to try to clear up a credit report because a credit card was used by someone at a place we never heard of. We still have businesses, like my doctor's office, who insist on using Social Security numbers to identify me, when they don't have to. Credit card thieves steal them from places like that. A woman used my credit card number to buy groceries in Texas. The credit card company called me and asked about that charge, within an hour of it being used. It was used four other times in that hour, so I got a new card. I'm thinking, "Why don't we have the cards like Europe has, that have chips in them so people can't make new cards from numbers they steal?" Is this loss and acceptable risk to a credit card company? They seem to be saying yes, and I seem to be saying no.

We have to decide: (1) do we protect everything the same, and do better at it, or (2) do we try to have a value proposition that works for a secret, no matter where it is? The implication of the former statement is the bulk of things that are part of the institutional databases will be protected the same. The latter, means we have a way of segregating data into pieces, we can all agree have a different value. We then put more control on the most valuable data, and less on everything else. We seem to have procedures in business and government that indicate we still believe we should be doing both, but we don't have enough resources to do both.

One glaring problem, making a policy difficult, is both government and the private sector see this as a different calculation. As long as they do, they will never agree. But, I don't think either of them is right.

In the government's classification system the value of a document is related to the amount of damage it would do to the national security of the United States, if disclosed to an unauthorized person [like somebody without a security clearance getting hold of it]. Top Secret is said to cause "exceptionally grave damage", Secret, "serious damage", and Confidential, if it existed, would be "damage". As you might imagine, this is difficult to firmly put a finger on, since the meanings of "exceptionally grave" and "substantial" are pretty close together. It might also depend on whether that "unauthorized person" was a Russian spy in a dress, or my neighbor who was over for dinner last weekend. Usually one person is not going to be much of a problem for anyone. We can offer that person some "incentives" to keep quiet. When numbers of people are involved, it is harder to handle. As you may remember, the government then does something called a "damage assessment" to see if the information should be kept a secret.

Business tends to see this as a value of the data and the loss of revenue, potential revenue, or liability (a kind of revenue loss) that comes from losing a secret. If it is a patented item, they can go to court, but even there they have to look at the potential cost of doing that and what they expect to gain from it. Credit card companies look at the total number of transactions they make money on, the total number of credit card thefts, the amount of uncollectable debt, and decide whether there really is a reason to go to those cards with chips in them. Is it really worth it?

If it is a trade secret, they may have no recourse at all, except to sue the person who lost it. Government and the private sector explain this differently, but both try to define the loss in terms of their liability for losing it. This may be a better way of characterizing any loss of data.

What they are really asking is "How are people going to view my duty to protect something, given the obvious loss of it to someone outside the business?" Credit card frauds are attacking the small businesses which can't protect themselves from good hackers. [128] So, owners of small businesses can improve their security by using big vendor cloud services, or hiring permanent security help. But, they aren't doing either one. Government and businesses follow the same general strategy.

Their first reaction is to deny the loss, and ignore the duty to protect any data. After that, they will deny that the information was disclosed to "too many" people. That would mean it is then public, and there would be no point in protecting it. It would also mean there might be some liability attached to not protecting it, that liability finger is pointing to a business we are responsible for. It is easier to argue, as the both government and the private sector have done, that there was only one Russian spy and her government probably didn't share it with a lot of other countries. We did not do any damage to the business by letting it get out of the door. Anyone with a brain can see the idiocy of this.

I was actually doing one damage assessment that was stopped because it was finding too many things that had been given to too many people who should not have had it. At the time, I said, "not again" because it happens so often. We were looking for a special compartment of information on a network where it was not supposed to be stored. Every time we reported a new find, the people who were in charge were unhappy and asked us to stop looking for more. Of course they stopped it before "too many" became enough that would require downgrading the classification, so now we will never know how many of those things were on that network.

I have done damage assessments for law firms and defense contractors where things went onto the Internet and the management response was "not very many people on the Internet saw it" or "it was removed immediately from the Internet". These are not believable statements to anyone, except by people who want to ignore loss of a secret that keeps them employed. This just means that there are quite a few secrets that everyone knows. When they leak, they continue to be secrets. We have to have changes in the law to make businesses liable for leaks of their data, similar to the way Europe does it.

WIKILEAKS has allowed people to see government and business secrets that they would never get to see otherwise, but none of them are Really Big Secrets. Most of these things are formal government secrets that are called SECRET, to distinguish then from things that are TOP SECRET. The Federal government has a *hierarchy* of secrets, with TOP SECRET ones being more important than SECRET ones.

Most companies do not have this type of problem, because the hierarchical model is too hard to figure out. They don't use it. That would seem to say that it is no longer true that information has a value that is different, depending on some criteria that we use to separate it. All of the WIKILEAKS government documents were SECRET, but a number of people thought they had nothing SECRET in them at all. Some in the State Department might think they were.

If I say the Kazakhstan Ambassador is having an affair with someone in the Turkish embassy, I don't want to see that on the front page of a newspaper, with my name as the originator. This is where truth doesn't count. Truth is a defense in law, but not politics. What this says is the value of the information is not measured by the formal criteria that we chose to apply to it to call it SECRET. So while we still have formal policies making things different classifications, the value isn't reflected in the designation. If we look at the same information in a private sector e-mail system, the value of it will still be the same. This is a secret with some political value, which is hardly ever evaluated in the formula for the risk of losing it.

WIKILEAKS has government secrets but they also have business secrets that are more competition sensitive than the government's, though both have the competition element. Just as one business competes with another, so do governments. WIKILEAKS said it would publish the contents of a banking executive's hard drive that would "bring down" a major U.S. bank.[129] That hasn't happened but it does have banks scrambling to see if might be them. A hard drive is going to be 300-500 Gigabits and that is more than a few book-length creations that could be about anything from those Cayman Islands operations to how Bob's wife is doing with the cancer she has. Even with half of it is taken up by software, there is a lot to read on one of them. If the files haven't been destroyed, as one of WIKILEAKS former employers said happened, then they can be as damaging to a bank as the cable traffic from the State Department was to our international dealings. I have to ask, "Where did they get a hard drive from a major U.S. bank, and why wasn't it missed?"

We need a way to decide how much they have been affected by losing something, so we can justify the expense of taking care of it. In business, this is called Return on Investment (ROI). How much is the content of any hard drive in a bank worth? We have to account for how much it will cost us to lose it, the odds of this happening, and what we have to do to protect all of the ones we have. There is quite a bit of speculation in these estimates and nobody is feeling good about putting some of these numbers up on a chart. There is always the chance that some new person will say, "Where does that number come from?" and there is no way to pull off an explanation. Using ROI does not work very well in the management of secrets, but that is still the way businesses try to do it. There is a quality aspect to the value of information that is more interesting and less able to be computed, the value of the duty to protect the data. Unfortunately, it is pseudo-science that allows us to believe that data value can be measured rationally.

The best example of that is the type of information that comes from whistleblowers, like Kyle Lagow, Greg Mackler[130] and

Cheryl Eckard[131]. The new provisions of the False Claims Act, where GlaxoSmithKline was prosecuted, allows whistleblowers to go to the Justice Department with information about potential wrongs companies may have done, and get part of the proceeds in a settlement. Lagow got $14.5 million dollars, enough to make any business nervous. The Federal Government got a $25 billion settlement from Bank of America ($25B seems to be a magic number here too). Cheryl Eckard got $96 million for her part in the investigation of GlaxoSmithKline, settled for $750 million. Yes, that is the same GlaxoSmithKline, being investigated again, one year later, which might indicate they have not learned a good lesson the first time around, or the lesson they did learn was the wrong one.

The numbers seem beyond imagination, but what do they really mean? Big numbers for little pieces of information do not seem to make sense, but we have values for secrets that everyone can relate to. They are big numbers, and they are likely to get bigger with the new Dodd-Frank provisions expanding whistleblower incentives. A one-paragraph e-mail can be worth a lot of money. Part of what this says is the quality of some data is greater than some others of a similar type and that quality is measured by what it represents – corruption, or other types of wrongdoing, of the worst kind. What they measure is the value of losing something that should be protected.

This may not be the lesson my readers would like businesses to have, but the truth is, secrets are secrets until they are given away to someone else, be that investigators with warrants, hackers, or newspapers. Had the companies that were indicted by the Justice Department kept their secrets, they could have saved that $25 Billion. Most corporations don't spend anywhere near that amount for data protection and leak investigations. My lesson for them is to spend more to protect secrets and less for fines. The real numbers that should be attached to something is the liability that comes from losing something the government or business has a duty to protect. That is a duty that should be the same, for the same types of information, in both government and business. This is what the cloud vendors in our Information Technology business areas are saying when they say they are not responsible for the data in a cloud. Storing it in China will not be our biggest problem, if we accept that business approach.

What they are missing is that every company has a duty to protect data it has in its possession, if for no other reason than to meet standards of due diligence for their management. The European approach to this is that any company requesting data from a person, has an obligation to protect it on behalf of that person, or words to that effect. This is a principle we established when computer security was new, but vendors have undermined over time. We have to have legislation to restore that principle. If a company stores my private data, they have to be responsible for protecting it.

128 See Symantec, *Internet Security Threat Report, 2013*, Symantec Corporation, page 4.

129 Nelson d. Schwartz, *Facing Threat from Wikileaks, Bank Plays Defense*, New York Times, 2 January 2011, http://www.nytimes.com/2011/01/03/business/03wikileaks-bank.html?_r=1&pagewanted=all

130 Nate Raymond, *DOJ Filings on $25 Billion Settlement Detail Whistleblower Claims*, Law.com, 15 March 2012, http://www.law.com/jsp/cc/PubArticleCC.jsp?id=1202545574699

131 Peter Loftus, *Whistleblower's Long Journey*, Wall Street Journal, 28 October 2010, http://online.wsj.com/article/SB10001424052702303443904575578713255698500.html

CHAPTER 12

....

A Mess Made in High Places

We have too many secrets for too many different reasons, and we are not protecting the ones we have. It may be true that most of different reasons are good reasons, but together, they add up to something that isn't. We have too much policy, and most of it should be thrown out. We started writing it when George Washington was President and it has been accumulating and adapting to technology for the entire time since. It has been folded, mashed and fluffed until it has the consistency of a soufflé. Now, we have a free-for-all that is not good for any of us. It has government bickering among itself, and the private sector fighting in court for every patent they can muster. We have too many secrets to keep our competitive edge, and some of them have not been secrets for a long, long time.

Dr. John Carroll, one of Canada's first computer security experts, told me that Americans are not good at writing policy because they always want to tell people what they can do, when they should be telling them what they can't. This makes shorter, tighter policy, and it works well for legislation too. Suppose we had one short law that said "personally identifiable information cannot be given to any third party" or words that lawyers can put together to say the same thing? Suppose we said that only one person in any Federal Agency has the ability to make something a really big secret? Focus our National Policy on making a few descriptions of what our government and businesses can do to make something a secret, and deal with it. The usual government approach to this is to form a commission and start plowing through all the laws until the general public forgets about the issue that started the whole thing. This isn't something that requires that kind of plodding.

Tomorrow, the President could issue a new Executive Order that would limit the number and type of things that could be national security information, the number of people in government who are allowed to dictate what is classified, and new declassification orders for those things that were already classified. Executive Orders are much easier to do, as this President found in immigration policy. The President decided to erase parts of immigration law by Executive Order and leave hundreds of thousands of people exempt from deportation even though they were here illegally. Information policy is even easier to do, but it works only for National Security Information, the Top Secret and Secret kind. He has to go through Congress for the rest.

Most of the protection of other types of information comes from law and not Executive Order. We have too many different laws trying to promote a category of information as something that needs to be protected when used with a particular industry or association. It is next to impossible to rewrite the number and types of legislation to focus on narrowing the laws and focusing them on information we are trying to protect.

Justice and Commerce Departments have a large role in controlling information that relates to export control and law enforcement, neither of which has been looked at in 50 years. With China stealing us blind, our Export Laws can't help us very much unless we do something about the stealing. We can't do export controls or law enforcement the way we did when Eisenhower was President, but that is how we are trying to do it today.

Patent and Trademark have a role in how patents are made and enforced. It is hard for anyone to believe that there can be a half a million unique things being invented every year, double what we had just a couple of years ago. We now think of a patent as an asset that is worth as much as manufacturing capability, but this is a problem government has created. Half of all U.S. patents are originated by foreign companies, and Japan is at the top of that list, not China. China is fourth, so the number and types of patent applications seem to have very little to do with the amount and type of trade being generated, or the innovation of the country where they orginate. China's resident patent applications are increasing faster than those of the U.S.[132] Patent wars have become common in the telecommunications sector, and we need to look at whether that is good or bad for the industries that make it up. In the meantime, we can expect more patents, not less.

In 2011, the Obama Administration passed the America Invents Act which changes patents in a fundamental way. It changes the filing of patents from first-to-invent, to first-to-file, a situation that benefits the large companies with lawyers who can review and file patents more easily than a small business. They also did away with a grace period that allowed small businesses to set up financing and testing of products before they filed for a patent.[133] With this gone, they now run the risk of missing a filing trying to keep a new idea secret. This moves patents into the haven of large businesses with clout.

The Commerce Department also is responsible for another area of law that is difficult to understand. The Arms Export Control policies are about as convoluted, vague and backward as any protection policies we have. The Arms Export Control Act started all of this and says that the President will designate a list of things that are defense articles and services. These are not necessarily classified, but can be, and include things like firearms, ammunition, launch vehicles for missiles, the missiles, rockets, torpedoes, explosives, "vessels of war"(ships that are used for sea battle), military electronics, guidance equipment, toxicological agents and radiological equipment. These are the kinds of things you would normally think of as war making. But, there are some other categories like "defense services not otherwise enumerated" and "miscellaneous articles" that lead to difficulties of interpretation. The intent is to discourage the sale of war-making materials to foreign governments that may use them against us. It doesn't stop companies from doing it, but they occasionally get caught and fined for not getting a license to export something. Our latest one of these was United Technologies (UTC), which makes most of its money selling defense items for *our* defense. [134] This incident showed up in the 2013 Defense Department annual report but happened in 2002 and 2003.

UTC managed to build a helicopter with military software in it and ship it over to China. The Army started using it in 2009. They knew it was going to be difficult to get a license from Canada where this part of UTC is located. The Canadian government is not too keen on giving the Chinese any help to build up their military. The Chinese cooperated by pointing out the civilian version of this helicopter and saying the export was really for that program. Both sides new better, but both sides went on anyway. According to the WSJ article, "In an email that the Justice Department said was sent on Sept. 12, 2001, Pratt Canada's export manager cautioned that the company had to be careful that the helicopter program with China not be presented as military. 'We need to be very careful with the Z10C program,' the email said, according to the deferred prosecution agreement. 'If the first flight will be with a gun ship then we could have problems with the US government.' That turned out to be an accurate statement. UTC admitted it and paid a $75M fine. That short e-mail was one expensive piece of information.

This is a big enough company to have an export manager and a staff to handle foreign sales. Imagine a small business trying to run this kind of sale and you see why so many small businesses can't keep up in the international markets. Sometimes, they know they are violating the law. The Chinese have found ways to take advantage of that.

The Chinese are using small companies which have some similar characteristics: they have naturalized citizens running them; the people who run these companies work for a company with some technology the Chinese want; a Chinese business arranges to buy that technology and get to it through a relationship with the small business; the small business does not own the technology they are selling; the Chinese don't care who really owns it. The Justice Department, to its credit, is starting to prosecute more and more of them.

Companies get around it by setting up research facilities in other countries and exporting their technologies through those. They can apply for licensing, but enforcement of those licensing agreements in foreign facilities is next to impossible. The U.S. can't regulate the development of technology in a foreign research facility. The goods produced are part of the economy of the country where it is taking place. It is good question as to whether these research facilities are good for the U.S. Dual use technologies make it difficult to see how a product might benefit a military, and we have companies that would cooperate in doing that even if they did. They may not even be good for the U.S. companies that sponsor them, but they are often conditions of operating in another country, especially China.

On the national security side, we should have fewer, more narrowly defined, things that are secret. This is a bad business because it will mean that some things that we think are dear to us are going to not be secrets anymore. Terrorists use almost anything we make available to them, so we increased the things our government will try to keep from them. Using this approach, terrorists will get more information about us, but less of the important things like the White House has been giving them over the last few years.

Fewer secrets make keeping the ones we have easier, but some policy changes are required to make that a practical reality. Our current policies favor keeping secrets forever because they require a review of material that was classified at the end of a predefined period. That review is impossible to do because of the volume of information that is being generated every day by our computer systems. The private sector doesn't have this problem, because there has to be some uniqueness to its data for it to be protected by patent or trade secret laws. The government doesn't require uniqueness to be considered when classifying something, but it is something they should consider.

Making Secrets to Keep

There is an old adage in the security business that says you must prevent what you can't detect, and detect what can't prevent. This is a simple idea that is rarely gets any attention, yet is it one of the best concepts we have for protecting secrets. If we can't prevent the loss of secrets by individuals working inside our government and commercial businesses, then we have to be able to detect it. The concept seems to have fallen in a crack between security of information systems, and management of sensitive information. We need to pull it out and start looking at it again.

We certainly know how to identify who is leaking information and bring charges against them when it is criminal. Some people may have a problem believing it, but there is a good amount of people in security, especially National Security, who know how to run a leak investigation to find out whether someone is leaking when we don't know for sure where, or how, it is happening. They may not be in the Justice Department, but they are out there. There are a few leak investigations going on at any given time, but the results are almost never published anywhere. They are usually internal because they will be embarrassing to the organization conducting them, so they become secrets in their own right. It takes time, and lots of legwork, but it can be done by anyone who really wants to stop leaking things. That may sound incredible because not very many government agencies or businesses run these types of programs to find out who is leaking. They don't look for leaks, so they never find them.

This reminds me of a CIO that we were briefing on the placement of network intrusion detection sensors on her network. We had spent months working with the IT staff on how the sensors were to be controlled, integrated and how the data from them would be analyzed. We were doing a final briefing on timing the installations so they wouldn't interfere with operations. I noticed a look on her face like she was seeing the sensor deployment for the first time and could not understand what we were doing. Since this was her third briefing, it bothered me that she didn't seem to understanding what I was telling her. I stopped my brief and asked her if she had a question. She looked annoyed and said, "I see what you are doing here and I don't like it. You can't be doing this." Her own staff was looking at one another and wondering what she was talking about. She then added, as an afterthought, "You will probably find things that are wrong and catching people who are doing things that might get us in trouble. I can't let this happen." I took this sentiment to my boss and she took it to hers.

In the end we got our sensors and her analysis proved to be correct. The first case we had was two people in the IT Department who were using the network to process batches of pornographic images for a number of other users. They were both fired from their jobs and she left the organization a short time later, to "seek other business opportunities", a phrase many know well. She was probably right that not knowing was better than knowing what was going on in her own network, and we have people in both government and business circles who would rather not have the publicity that comes from finding people doing wrong. If they just started doing wrong last Tuesday, their managers might be forgiven, but that is not usually the case. They have been doing it for months or years and should have been discovered long ago. They would have, if any one bothered to look.

In the early 90's I was on a project in the IRS to find tax processors who were accessing tax records they were not allowed to have. Tax records are divided into alphabetical sections and processors are only allowed to see a section of them, so a person might be limited to tax payers with names beginning A-C. Our group was working on an audit analysis program that looked for violations of the policy. It was simple and easy for everyone to understand, but the analysis took time and was being done from years of records, so it was slow. We picked a Region in the IRS to test it on, and took our equipment to Atlanta to get the data from their audit system. The program ran for several weeks, chugging away in a back office that was not connected to the network. It didn't bother anyone.

The results identified several hundred potential cases, most of them just one or two times that a person might have looked for a name outside the group assigned. Sometimes they were checking on themselves, a potential spouse, a famous person, or a relative. Most of those were not serious and we didn't even consider them disciplinary matters. But there were some others that were different. Of the 250 cases, about 10 were accessing quite a few people every year who were not in their assigned cases. A couple of them were into the hundreds of times a year that they were doing it. Those few, we turned over to the internal investigations part of IRS. One person, it turns out, was selling information about tax records of famous and wealthy people to magazines. He was criminally prosecuted and this was in all the papers in Atlanta. A couple of others were helping him. The vast majority of the cases were handled by internal reprimands and warnings, but the ones that made the papers made the IRS Atlanta Region look tainted.

After the smoke settled, we had a formal meeting with our own leaders in the IRS Headquarters and we got to listen to some of the comments made by the political factions in Atlanta and the ones in Washington. They were livid about the results. They did not want a repeat of the audits done there and asked us to close down the audit program and declare it a success. We were not to give the software or equipment to any of the other IRS Regions. We never saw our own equipment after that. They didn't want to look again, for fear of what they might find. We were not looking at groups applying for tax-exempt status. This was simple, by comparison.

The rationale for not looking can sound pretty good. It is expensive to look. There probably is not much leaking going on, because we haven't had this type of problem come up before. Finding someone leaking might cause us to be looked at more closely by regulators or other government agencies. We have no reason to believe it is happening now. We trust our employees. We might have to do some things that we really don't want to do to discover a leak. Anyone who has ever done this kind of work, has heard other excuses. We could have a whole Dilbert series on these types of things.

The other side of this issue is that we may not be able to do what is required to stop leaks from happening. Somebody with a moral compass is going to try to upset our whole operation.

Our CIO understood this very well. She knew those sensors were going to detect things that were under her control and she would be required to respond. With her own bureaucratic reasoning, she thought not having them identified to begin with was better than allowing sensors to monitor the system. We had momentum on our side, because we had invested months of work on this, but if she had raised objections in the beginning, it might have been harder to get our monitoring started. She could claim, as others did afterwards, that we were violating someone's privacy by checking who they sent mail to. People don't like to be watched, even though every computer in a business or government agency clearly says it is subject to monitoring. That is what we were doing, and we made it more difficult to criticize by not looking at content of documents. We just looked at connections being made (yes, metadata), but that didn't stop some, including the Army General Counsel, from saying it was a violation of an individual's privacy to monitor in that way.

Boeing was criticized for reading its employees' mail (and there was some question about whether they were really reading or just finding out where it was going) but the employees were using a Boeing system to get access to it. A company can use information that goes through its own systems in prosecuting a case, even where attorney-client relationships were established. [135] They can read your mail. A company can do lots of things that are legal, but they often don't. It doesn't matter what they do, because someone will criticize, no matter what path a business takes.

Good monitoring can help, but it doesn't always show what wrongdoers are up to. The use of informants in law enforcement or criminal investigations is often the only way of getting an inside view of what is going on behind the scenes, but these kind of informants are not generally loved by anyone. The are called "snitches" in many places, and worse things in gangs and organized crime. Criminal organizations go out of their way to look for, and deal with, people who inform on them and they use some of the same methods law enforcement and business would use on criminals, to discover them.

In those cases, law enforcement already has a pretty good idea of where and how the crime is being committed, but they don't have any eyewitnesses, or much evidence. Eichenwald titled his book *The Informant,* because that is the only way some crimes can be exposed. The difference in this type of situation is the knowledge that something is going on inside the company that is illegal and that is presented to law enforcement to collect evidence.

Informants are used extensively in research where subjects who are being interviewed are not likely to be truthful, without some protection of their identities and company affiliations[136]. We do this kind of research all the time in marketing and business intelligence, but we don't think about it as being a bad thing. The principle is almost exactly the same. Auditors and investigators already know that businesses lie to them and try to cover things up. They know that they have to have reliable sources that will be protected from company reprisals.

In debates over how to lessen the chance that some worker in a data center would take data from the people it was serving, Willis Ware, from RAND suggested there were quite a few possible solutions, including one that raised eyebrows – a business could put an informant in every data center. But, he added, they might not be able to live with the consequences of doing it, even though it could be done. If the informant were to be discovered, how would the employees feel about having someone inside doing something like this? It is not the way we see ourselves in the U.S. unless we are building something like the new atom bomb. We are certainly never going to put informants in the workplace, to protect a secret. Never may be too strong a word here. This is the dilemma with detection of secrets that are being leaked. We don't like what has to be done to protect ourselves. I'm not suggesting that we put informants everywhere, but let's understand why we need to use them and make informed decisions about where they are used.

Can a business or government agency monitor the content of company e-mail of any of its employees? Can they monitor every keystroke a person makes? Can they monitor telephone calls made on company cell phones? Can they put cameras in workplaces to monitor what employees are doing? Can they establish policies that prohibit employees from talking to competitors unless approved business relationships? Can they embed tracking software in documents and track where those documents go, even to a home computer used for business? Can they put dummy files on a computer so they will trigger an alarm if they are e-mailed from the facility? Can they put RFI devices on company equipment that track when they enter and leave a building? Can they give employees information that is "made up" to track how that flows to potential places outside? Can they limit contacts with the press? Can they ask an employee to take a polygraph examination? I have to say that we have the law on our side here. We can do all of these things to find out if someone is leaking, but it goes against our nature. Most of the time, those restrictions are self-imposed.

When there are only six government prosecutions for the epidemic release of classified information about on-going national security programs, and that is considered an improvement over previous administrations, we are living in a time when governments don't hold anyone accountable for speaking out on things that are classified. The Justice Department appointed two internal lawyers to investigate the White House leaks, so we don't have to have a second thought about what they will find, or when. Now that the election is over, they might even try to interview a few people who were present in those meetings where the secrets were given to the press and print journalists. But we don't have to look very far for a better example of leaking and the failure of our government agencies to prosecute.

We have the classic case of this with the publication, in September 2012, of the book *No Easy Day*, by Matt Bissonnette, which describes the operations of the Seal Team that killed Osama Bin Laden. He says there wasn't any classified information in the book, but by his own account, he didn't have it reviewed prior to it being published, so there is no way to tell if the DoD people thought so.

The Defense Department is trying to decide whether to sue Bissonnette in civil court and take the money he gets for his book, because he didn't get it approved prior to publication. They have started laying the foundation for that type of action. Not having it approved is a violation of his secrecy agreement with Defense, but it hardly a substitute for identifying what is classified about that operation and prosecuting him for publishing that. Their unwillingness to go any further seems to say that book is not classified, or Defense has other reasons for wanting the book published.

Has anyone said that the Bissonnette interview on 60 Minutes, or the book, is classified? So far, only one person in Defense has said any such thing, at least in public. Do I think it might be classified? It doesn't matter what I think or what Bissonnette thinks. I loved his book and his interview but the censorship agreement with the government says it has to be reviewed before it is published. I do that review for my books and it is not hard. *No Easy Day* is written as a factual account of a Top Secret, covert military operation. The Defense Department, together with the Obama Administration, are playing a game that will make future operations more difficult and dangerous. They are also setting a precedent for how we make and keep secrets.

Contrast the government's ability, with our industrial systems, which also have not done very well at identifying and prosecuting leakers, though much better than government[137]. The problem for business is the number and types of cases is very small and, only rarely, significant. Most of the better known cases have been given to the government for prosecution by businesses that are affected; some are handled as administrative matters or go to civil court. A friend of mine is in forensics and works for a number of Washington businesses. Presented with the evidence from a forensics analysis, most of the people being investigated will admit to what they did. They may even agree to a settlement that doesn't allow them to be criminally prosecuted. Some will even agree to pay restitution. But even with forensics evidence, it may be hard to manage an incident so secrets aren't told through the press. It is better to make sure they never get there.

Tides verses the Boeing Company is probably one of the best examples since it establishes precedent for many others who might want to raise objections to how things are being done inside a company[138] and defines when a person is a whistle blower.

In 2007, two employees of Boeing found what they thought were discrepancies in the way Boeing did its internal audits. Since they were from the Sarbanes-Oxley Group in Boeing, the kind of audits they would have been doing were related to internal controls over financial documents and the procedures for making sure they were accurate. The employees claimed that tensions were high in the SOX Audit group upon their arrival in January 2007 because their management thought that Deloitte & Touche might declare a "material weakness" in the company's internal controls. They claimed Boeing pressured IT Sarbanes-Oxley auditors to rate Boeing's internal controls as "effective" and fostered a generally hostile work environment.

Their primary concern related to Boeing's use of PriceWater-houseCoopers contractors in the internal auditing of the company's IT controls. Tides and Neumann, the two employees, repeatedly complained to management about the practice of giving these contractors managerial authority over Boeing employees, particularly since it related to how software was designed that looked at the internal controls. They complained about this often, but nothing much happened that they could see. When a reporter for the local newspaper, the Seattle Post-Intelligencer, contacted them, it moved off in a different direction. The newspaper published articles about Boeing that alleged employees' personal Google e-mail accounts were read and personnel were followed from the company, both things Boeing could legally do under the specific circumstances. Employees don't like it and some people outside of Boeing object to what was done, but there are two sides to every story like this.

The employees claimed protection as whistleblowers, and four years later and long after their dismissal from Boeing, they lost that case. It was clear that Boeing had the law on its side. Had Tides and Neumann gone to government regulators with the matters at hand, and let them decide whether to prosecute Boeing, their outcome might have been different, but they couldn't claim leaking information to the press was going help in prosecution of wrongdoing. In the previous cases in this book, the informants all went to the government agencies responsible for enforcement and got whistleblower protection, such that it is.

Boeing has to have a way of protecting itself from employee leaks, and not just from these two employees. They have thousands of employees who have access to an equal number of secrets. Some of the trade secret ones, if given out, are lost forever. Boeing has to be able to protect that information and they certainly have the means to do it, given the workplace laws that support them.

Privacy advocates will see the results differently, but the importance to national security lies in protecting Boeing's secrets and
not their employees' privacy. Boeing was engaged in lawful activity and was trying to protect its rights.

What this says to businesses is the same thing WIKILEAKS
publications said to the State Department. The value of a secret,
especially one that describes something "bad" that a business or
government is doing, is much higher than the average person
believes. In risk calculation, it is called exposure to liability and
it relates to that "probability of occurrence" in the risk formula.
Most people carry this kind of liability because they are unable,
or unwilling, to deal with a simple part of secrets. There are only
a very few secrets that expose a government or business to disaster, but finding them is really hard, maybe impossible, to do. But
someone knows about them, and there has to be outlets to get the
information to the right people or it will be exposed another way.

There is no hierarchy for secrets like the formula for Coca-
Cola, but there is one for the things needed to protect that secret.
There is only one formula for Coke. The formula for Coca-Cola
actually has to be used, so it has to be given to a quite few people.
We all know that the more people that have a secret, the greater
chance that secret will eventually get out. That is where compartmenting a program can be a benefit. Not everyone gets all of the
formula at one time. Coke might have some of the formula premade so that adding a few things to it make it complete, but the
people doing the adding don't know what the premade part of it
actually is. They could take it to a laboratory and break it down
into its chemical parts but some of the process that puts Coke
together might be not be obvious from the chemicals in it. Those
non-obvious parts of the processing cycle need to be compartmented too. They probably want to keep track of the people who
have access to the special processing sections and the premade

portion of the formula to make sure they don't sell this part to the Chinese. The total of the things that are done to protect the formula will be collected somewhere at the top of the company and a description of what is being done will be the most important document that Coca-Cola has, outside of the actual formula itself. So another aspect of secrets is the methods of protecting a secret can be just as important as the secret itself. We would have to admit they have done a pretty good job of protecting it since 1886 when it came to be.[139]

Clouded up in all those Really Big Secrets are quite a bit of things that are Not Very Secret and a person new to the business will not know the difference between them. WIKILEAKS was a good example of the kind of thing that is SECRET. The New York Times and the Guardian had selectivity about the WIKILEAKS documents they published, i.e. they could choose what to publish and only publish the most interesting things.[140] They had to filter through all the stuff that comes in from hundreds of other people who have whole lives centered around production of "products" that are usually nothing more than pieces of information from other writers who have to produce their products. They are like reporters for newspapers and magazines, writing and rewriting things over and over until we are all tired of hearing and seeing so much on the same subject that we turn it off, literally. An editorial staff can sympathize with the average government person who does the same thing every day, trying to find a terrorist that the President can put on that target list.

That is not a good thing. The 9/11 Commission published a huge report that described why it was that the government was not able to "connect the dots" and this seemed to stick with people everywhere. It seems easy enough. If you have a bunch of dots that represent some type of action being taken by a terrorist group, it is easy to draw lines between those dots and produce a picture. Everyone will then see clearly what is happening and can rush to save our country from another disaster.

I spent many, many hours behind a screen of a computer searching for dots and there are as many as the searches you can make, and for each type of search, a different set of them. Try this yourself, using more than one search engine and see what results there will be. There are so many dots that you can never see them all, let alone connect them. There are too many of them. Everything we do to find terrorists is a secret; everything the terrorists do is a secret; everything we know about how they do things is a secret. Endless secrets. And, this only covers one set of secrets, those we have about terrorists. There are a lot more, where those came from. Our ability to make things secret and keep them secret has gotten out of hand. When everything is a secret, it is hard to keep a secret safe.

In both *No Easy Day* and Watergate, the public version of events was different than the one being offered by the White House and that may have been the key to how they were resolved. If Defense wanted the real story to be told, they would have to make it less painful for anyone who would risk telling it. We have the White House helping to make a movie about the same incident. The two don' t make a good picture of our inclination to protect secrets of any kind. We should do more to make leaking harder.

Every agency and business pretends like it audits its employees every hour of every day and can tell in a second what they are up to. That is wishful thinking, at best. Auditing has been around since computers were invented and almost never found anyone stealing anything other than computer time. Occasionally, people do real estate, buying, selling, and making pornography, and a few other crimes of various sorts, but auditors rarely find what we think they should. There are too many servers and paths into and out of a network to follow them all. There are over 300 billion e-mails sent every day, to somebody, and there are text messages, social media and telephone calls that would have to be monitored too. It is not possible. Not just hard to do, not possible, to monitor everyone doing everything on their computers at work, or at home. There are a few legal issues attached to it too that make it more difficult, but there is no point in covering all of those to make the same point. So, we cannot detect it, and with our current technology, we cannot prevent it.

We can't detect it using traditional computer security without doing much better auditing than we are capable of doing in most places; neither government nor business seem willing to pay for it. We can detect leaks with programs that are especially designed to find people who are leaking information, but that may require us to do a few things, particularly surveillance, we are not willing to do. We are not going to stop leaking by any computer related means as long as both of these things are true. If we look at Apple's original case against Samsung, the issue was that Apple had not completed an investigation to determine where the leaks were coming from. It has to start there.

It certainly won't be detected right away. Transferring data to a mobile device or from a computer at home adds a step that can't be monitored as easily as we would believe. Spying, leaking and insider trading is harder to detect because the information is not going directly to a person who may end up with it. If it is also encrypted, it is going to be very hard to find. To find leaks requires some ability to see through both the technology making leaking easier, and limiting the number and types of secrets so we don't have to monitor everyone or everything. We have the law and technical ability to do it, but we don't. That unwillingness is hurting us.

Too Many Secrets

Part of our reluctance is the inability to cut back on the making of secrets. We have a lot of things that are, when held up the light, not as classified, sensitive, or important as we thought when making them. Those reduce the credibility of things that really are. If we were more careful about the secrets we made, our businesses and government could protect less data.

After 9/11, we decided limiting the exchange of secrets was a core problem for our government agencies and we tried to repair that condition by making more secrets that could be shared. That being government logic, nobody even flinched at the idea. What we should have done is make fewer secrets and protect the ones we have. Things that are not secrets are easily shared, but that certainly does not apply to covert programs.

The whole idea behind covert programs is their secrecy and deniability. The process of establishing and operating them is wrapped up in secrecy that everyone involved with is supposed to understand and agree to. We can't have newspapers and book publishers being given information that tells the world's readers what is being done in our most sensitive programs. In most of the programs I worked on, nobody in our operations ever thought of writing a book about what we were doing, and how we were doing it, until the programs were public.

I interviewed a woman who had been on the Manhattan project that produced the first atomic bomb. This is the kind of secret that the military has to keep and is the difference between winning and losing a war. We have very few secrets that will ever be this important, but without a doubt, we have many more than the public knows about.

She never told her parents or Uncle what she was working on, because she didn't actually know. When the first bomb went off over Nagasaki, Japan, she had a feeling that the people in her office were involved. She was smart enough to figure out some of the things that were going on- especially travel to the desert Southwest. She knew the types of people she was working with, their skills sets, and where that work was being done. She figured it was a weapon, because there was an active war on, but didn't know what kind or how significant a thing it would be. Of course, nobody knew anything about atomic bombs then, except scientists who were working on them.

The people in the office didn't usually talk to one another about work, unless it was necessary. Outside the office, they didn't compare notes very often because they knew that the Germans and Japanese were interested in the work they were doing, without having them stop by and ask questions. They became very secretive and some of them found it so stressful, they went to other jobs rather than work there. Some of them were removed and nobody knew why.

She had worked across the isle from a man who was nice and worked as hard as she did and when they exploded those bombs in Japan, she saw him the next day in an Army uniform. He was there to make sure they didn't talk about their work, an informant so to speak. But, he also did other things that were certainly not democratic, nor were they intended to be. He monitored their mail and business transactions and kept records on a few people. She didn't even know that was happening. In the end, she was glad it was over because keeping those kinds of secrets was hard work and made a person paranoid. But, these are the kinds of things that have to be done to keep a secret like the one they had.

In my days with really secret programs, I never wondered about whether we could keep them secure long enough to use what we were producing. I'm not sure about anything today. I asked her, in 1977, if we could run a Manhattan project, with all the computers and communications that we had, and she said, "I doubt it. We couldn't live with the kind of restrictions that we had to have to keep all those things secret." In 2014, it is a thousand times more difficult to do than it was then.

We are all connected to reporters, writers, friends, relatives and social media friends. We feel like we know these people and we don't have reasons to not trust them. Yet, my granddaughter says, "Be careful who you talk to on-line." Her little face was so serious.

Maybe it is because her mother knows there are sexual predators out there with our friends, or maybe she is just smarter than some of the rest of us. I wonder if she knows there are spies and criminals out there too. We trust too many people with secrets who should not have them. We no longer have a sense that there are secrets that are worth that kind of effort that kept the secret of the first Atomic Bomb, and, we have the means to tell anyone we want about every secret we know. One day this will be our end.

On the flip side of this, the government is not moving fast enough to declassify anything. They stick it in computers and keep it Top Secret forever. They don't work at downgrading it to a lower level to make it more accessible to others in government, nor do they think of declassifying it. They use this to cover up programs that didn't work very well or ones that went further than their charters allowed.

Given the bulk of things stored in computers today, there is nothing in print that is not classified in some context in some database maintained by an agency somewhere in the world. A person cannot say much of anything that someone in government would not say was classified in some context. This is ridiculous.

Businesses are not protecting their secrets very well, and adopting business practices that make them rich in the short run, but undermine the value of their intellectual property, or risk losing it entirely. The shareholders need to pay more attention to it. They file millions of patents every year, not because they need to, but because they believe they can't protect themselves without them. The opposite is true. The patents don't help them when people steal those ideas and counterfeit their own products. They ignore their patents. We see this every day in our relations with China, Russia, and every third world country that makes counterfeits of U.S. goods.

What the Chinese haven't stolen from us in industrial espionage, we have given them through business arrangements that make technology exchange a given part of the relationship. It should not be a surprise that the Chinese then compete with us in the same areas, because that is what giving then research does. It makes them more competitive. This ridiculous idea is hardly ever attacked by shareholders because they see short-term profits as a good thing.

The Chinese have State Secrets that they protect almost any way they can, including making something a business like Rio Tinto had collected, a State Secret after-the-fact. It is like me telling General Motors that the data they collected on satisfaction of Ford and Toyota truck owners was Top Secret and sanction them for having it. This is cheating by most business standards, but the Chinese don't regard anything their businesses do as cheating. They believe it is competition and they are allowed to compete anyway they can. Anything is "fair trade".

The Chinese make their business secrets State secrets because their businesses are owned by the State. They use the justification that they are State secrets to control them on the Internet, but they are building up an overhead in protection that will be hard to maintain. We won't do that, and have no desire to mix the two except in things related to national defense. We shouldn't have to convince business leaders to make secrets needed to protect an advantage; they should know that their businesses survive on the ability to keep a strategy away from competitors. Maybe business schools aren't teaching that anymore.

We have a few business leaders who say, "no problem" to this idea because we can out-innovate any other country in the world. The Democrats even made that approach part of their election strategy. On an even playing field, there is some truth to that, but the Chinese have slanted it more than a little using economic warfare as a matter of national policy. They steal from us on a level that has caused the Secretary of the Treasury to remind Americans that the Chinese are stealing us blind. Richard Clarke has been saying that they have stolen secrets from every business in the U.S. They have certainly tried to do that, whether they were 100% successful or not. They counterfeit goods, the latest having a business impact on a company called Ubiquiti Networks, which lost 35% of it stock value when it underestimated the amount of counterfeiting of its devices marketed through a U.S. company, but manufactured in China. How does a company like Ubiquiti deal with something that is far outside their ability to contain? It isn't a lack of our innovation; it's a country of thieves, tolerated and encouraged by their government. We can't out innovate that kind of national conspiracy; we have to protect ourselves from it.

That means making secrets that are things we need to protect and keeping our secrets from people who shouldn't have them. Our past policies on Export Controls and Patents are not working very well in a world that tolerates stealing and forces research and development into trade agreements.

Since the end of World War II, nobody has seriously looked at how we make and keep secrets, though there are a stream of new Executive Orders that pretend to. It is a hard problem to break down and it is a harder problem now, than it was then. In The War, we were fairly sure what kind of secrets were needed, and the steps we had to go through to protect them. There were no easy ways to get paper documents out of a safe and into the hands of the Germans or Japanese. Our policies are made for those times.

Now, we are automated more than we should be, usually in the name of being "connected". Imagine what it would have been like to fight a World War II in our age of Bring Your Own Device (BYOD) to work. We can bring cell phones, tablets, and laptops and plug-in to our corporate and government networks, sometimes even when there are rules against it. We take them overseas and use them for business and battle. We might wonder how long it would have taken the Japanese to find our carrier groups in Midway if the cell phones of a few sailors were beaming out the location.

The Army has finally encouraged smartphone use by making one of its own.[141] Up until now, soldiers used theirs, sometimes to do things that are soldier-like, but not combat related. They text their sweethearts and wives, occasionally, with sexually explicit accompaniments. They talk to their children over Skype and Google Plus. Is there a censor around for any of this? Nobody even mentions the term anymore. They even text each other, and their leadership, sometimes expressing views directly to a high level leader. The term "chain of command" is dwarfed by the ability of soldiers and sailors to communicate directly with almost anyone, including their Congressional representatives and chat groups.

Cell phones are so widely abused in the business workplace, that records are commonly requested when accidents occur. Lisa Guerin describes the nature of cell phone abuse in her book *Smart Policies for Workplace Technologies,* telling of abuses of company phones, work time reporting, storing proprietary data on them, and using them for sensitive negotiations where more security is required. People abuse texting and e-mail, video recording, voice recording, and cameras. We can barely think about keeping secrets with these types of devices around. More and more, even business sees a need to restrict the use of phones, smartphones, and wearable technologies, like Google Glass, the mobile computer. They know there is liability there.

These kinds of devices take us back to our roots in keeping secrets. There are some secrets that used to only be communicated verbally, and in person. Those are the Really Big Secrets that float around in every hallway of almost every government and commercial office. Technology is supposed to work for us, not threaten our National Security, but there is a little of each going on these days. We haven't yet learned to discriminate between secrets we can't protect, or detect the loss of, and do better at keeping those. Neither politics, nor position, should affect our focus on this.

We seem to have forgotten that satellites are up in the outer reaches of our atmosphere listening to everything we say, and e-mail. We would not be content, even if only the U.S. were listening. There are about 1046 satellites in orbit belonging mostly to China, Russia and the U.S. but a few belong to Iran, India, Israel and 35 other countries and half of those are communications satellites.[142] Only some of these are listening, but we have no idea how many of those there are or who is doing it. In the near future, other countries will have them, because China has made a business for itself launching them for others. They even lease satellites to the U.S. military for use in Africa.[143]

We need to do better are using and controlling technologies that are sapping us of secrets. Part of this is just education of people who use computers and cell phones but part of it is the Telecommunications industry being unwilling to make their circuits more secure from eavesdropping. They would argue discussing secrets on electronic devices is the problem, and the circles would never connect. We really need some of each side to be more successful.

But, this is both a workplace and personal thing. At the personal level we have lost the ability to keep a secret. The electronic gadgets are part of it, but a generation ago, a secret could be kept because it was the right thing to do. I remember the whispered tones of my mother and her card-playing contemporaries talking about the pregnancy of a single woman who lived down the street from us. I wasn't even sure what they were talking about, but the secret was one they didn't want to share with the other tables of card players. Most of them probably got the news, eventually. That single piece of news is now Twittered and Facebooked to hundreds of "friends" we don't know anymore. The neighborhood is now far away. We really don't know how to keep a secret. Harmless, some people say, but I don't think so.

Both in business and government, the keeping of secrets is important to our ability to compete and be competitive, two different things. We compete as businesses and as a country with some really rough characters that want to win more than we do. What separates us from them, most of the time, is we are smarter than they are – more innovative, creative, adaptable, and most of all, free. At a personal, business and national level, what keeps us ahead of the rest of the world is secrets.

Nobody is immune from the running mouth, or e-mail-assisted booboo, "Reply to All". A woman talking, to a teenager in our grocery store said, "E-mail is forever." I lost one of my best security architects when a low-level administrator sent and attachment of an e-mail containing the salaries of every one of the people on his contract. He had the lowest salary, and accurately observed "There are some complete idiots over here who make more money than I do." He left and is making more than all of us now, proving his point.

Maybe we should have sympathy for those companies that thought reporting their overseas subsidiaries was too hard to do, because on top of all the other reporting that has to be done, it might be. Commercial healthcare is having the same problem with government over how much information the government thinks it needs to run commercial parts of Obamacare. They want information that no commercial operation is required to submit. The government has gotten itself into commercial business and does not know very much about how that is supposed to be done. This is part of an idea that it is OK to collect information for any reason, and share it with anyone who "needs" it.

At the same time, we have to run faster than the rest to stay ahead of anyone else who can run. That is becoming harder to do. We run trade deficits of over $30 Billion a month and we can't be feeling good about that. A huge part of that is money we should be taking in from our ability to innovate. We have ideas and those ideas are, essentially, given away – stolen away, in some cases. As a country, we have to do better, and we can. The real need is to focus on how we manage information in ways that allow it to be used, while protecting what is really important.

At the University of Wisconsin there was a plaque on the wall that proposes each person "sift and winnow" facts for himself before deciding what truth is. I always tell my students that they should not believe what they read, without checking for themselves. Look at the consequences of leaks of classified National Defense information, business information, and decide whether they affect us in ways we don't think much about. Look at the way we make secrets that both the Federal government and business leaders are supposed to protect. Does the way we are doing it now make sense? Is there a better way? Can we live with what we have to do to keep secrets? We should be able to answer all of these questions while we still have secrets worth keeping.

---

132 The World Intellectual Property Organization, *2011 Intellectual Property Indicators*, 2011, page 20.

133 America Invents Act of 2011: Good or Bad for Small Businesses? AriLaw, http://www.arilaw.com/blog/2012/01/america-invents-act-of-2011-good-or-bad-for-small-business/, accessed August 15, 2012

134 Kate Linebaugh, UTC Helped China Build First Military Attack Copter, Wall Street Journal, June 28, 2012 http://online.wsj.com/article/SB1000142405270230364 95045774947837276664496.html

135 For a broader discussion of some of these issues see, Catherine J. Lanctot, Attorney-Client Relationships in Cyberspace: The Peril and the Promise, Duke University Law Library, http://scholarship.law.duke.edu/cgi/viewcontent.cgi?article=1060&cont ext=dlj&sei

136 Nirmalya Kumar, Louis W. Stern, James C. Anderson, *Conducting Interorganizational Research Using Key Informants*, The Academy of Management Journal, Vol. 36, No. 6 (Dec., 1993), pp. 1633-1651 http://www.dedoose.com/_Assets/PDF/Publications/Kumar et al_1993_Key Informants.pdf

137 *The Leaky Corporation*, The Economist, 24 February 2011, http://www.economist.com/node/18226961

138 Katz, Marshall, and Banks, *Supreme Court Lets SOX Media Leaks Ruling Stand*, Sarbanes-Oxley Whistleblower Blog, 1 November 2011, http://www.sarbanes-oxley-whistleblower.com/blog/2011/11/01/supreme-court-won%E2%80%99t-hear-case-finding-media-contacts-not-protected-by-sox/; http://www.ca9.uscourts.gov/datastore/opinions/2011/05/03/10-35238.pdf

139 William Lee Adams, *Is This the Real Thing? Coca-Cola's Secret Formula 'Discovered'*, Time Newsfeed, 15 February 201, http://newsfeed.time.com/2011/02/15/is-this-the-real-thing-coca-colas-secret-formula-discovered/

140

141 Brendan McGarry, Army Set to Introduce Smartphones in Combat, Wired, 27 March 2013, http://www.military.com/daily-news/2013/03/27/army-set-to-introduce-smartphones-into-combat.html

142 Nirmala Ganapathy, *India Launches 7 Satellites in One Go*, The Strait Times, February 26, 2013 and United Nations Report, *Satellite Debris*, June 2008.

143 Tony Capaccio, *Pentagon Continues Use of China Satellite in New Lease*, Bloomburg, 15 May 2013.

EPILOGUE

If there was ever a need for secrets, it would be in the places that produce our most important weapon systems for the military, but since those are important secrets, they are some of the best targets for people after them. Apparently, the Chinese have been successful at stealing some of the best secrets these defense contactors have. When anyone steals from a contractor, they are taking secrets that belong both to the government, such as contacting strategies, units being purchased, problems identified by the government that pertain to how the product is being manufactured, and the proprietary designs and processes of the contractor. These are the life's blood of National Security.

The Defense Science Board has published a "confidential" report that says several of our largest and most important, defense contractors, like Lockheed Martin, Raytheon, and Northrop Grumman, none of whom would acknowledge they were hacked.[144] The targeted areas included the Aegis radar and missile defense modifications, the Patriot Missile System, the Terminal High Altitude Area Defense System, The F/A 18 Fighter, the V-22 Vertical Take Off Osprey, the Navy's new Littoral Ship, and the F-35 Fighter which was said to have been hacked in 2007. The total number of defense programs was said to be in the dozens and a list can be found in a link to reference 1 in this section. The Chinese must really need missile defense to steal this much related to it.

First, there are two paragraphs in this newspaper article that deserve a direct quote:

1. In January, the advisory panel warned in the public version of its report that the Pentagon is unprepared to counter a full-scale cyber-conflict. The list of compromised weapons designs is contained in a confidential version, and it was provided to The Washington Post.

2. A spokesman for the Pentagon declined to discuss the list from the science board's report. But the spokesman, who was not authorized to speak on the record, said in an e-mail, "The Department of Defense has growing concerns about the global threat to economic and national security from persistent cyber-intrusions aimed at the theft of intellectual property, trade secrets and commercial data, which threatens the competitive edge of U.S. businesses like those in the Defense Industrial Base."

So, somebody sent the Washington Post newspaper a list of compromised weapons designed that were contained in a report that was not for public release, and a spokesman, who is not authorized to speak on the record for the Department, writes on the record anyway. He didn't say much of any importance, but this is similar to the person who conspires to fix prices but doesn't make any money at it. He is not likely to be prosecuted for saying very little.

Second, we are losing so much information about sensitive defense programs that some of the biggest and most sophisticated parts of the inventory are being taken from under our collective noses, right out of the very defense contractors who make them. It is apparent that neither business or government secrets are being kept very well. There is a certain amount of irony here since most of these contractors advertise their computer security capabilities on the Internet to their defense customers. We should expect better from them.

Third, the Defense Science Board does not blame the Chinese, but the Obama Administration has taken actions to warn the Chinese anyway. It is difficult to believe that the Board did not have access to the types of intelligence that would allow them to say whether the Chinese were behind it or not, and if we look for the usual suspects, there aren't very many who could use this much information in any useful way. There is plenty of evidence around that they were responsible, and the Administration would appear to think so. The Chinese deny it, as we have come to expect. There is more to come.

In May of 2013, the Justice Department announced it had issued a warrant in 2010, and shared classified information, with the recipients of the warrant, for information pertaining to the activities of Stephen Jin-Woo Kim. Mr. Kim works for the State Department and will soon be in well-known, judging from the extent of this investigation. The released letter contains the subject of certain types of evidence that were seized and what among that was to be shared, in with the law firm. During discovery the government and the law firm would identify, as carefully as possible, what information they would use in court to show the guilt or innocence of a client. That part is fairly routine in criminal cases, but some of that information included the telephone numbers of certain exchanges related to Fox News, and five reporters.[145] Most news stories have mentioned only one.

The President of the United States made a statement critical of the way this was done, saying:

> "As Commander-in Chief, I believe we must keep information secret that protects our operations and our people in the field. To do so, we must enforce consequences for those who break the law and breach their commitment to protect classified information....But a free press is also essential for our democracy. That's who we are, and I'm troubled by the possibility that leak investigations may chill the investigative journalism that holds government accountable."[146]

Neither the press, nor the Justice Department are telling the whole story but both are indignant about what the other has said about it. [147] This is not a leak investigation, by the looks of it.

Neither side has publically said what Kim has been charged with, though a few newspapers mention the release of a specific report about North Korean nuclear capabilities. The discovery letters indicate there is a good deal more than that involved. The government seized the unclassified hard drives, his personal Apple computer, and the Top Secret hard drive of Mr. Kim's computers at the State Department. They also had a hard drive from a laptop that Kim had at the Department of Energy, several years before that. Two referenced seizures were emails he sent in 2005. They did traps on several phone numbers at several different vendors, Comcast, Verizon, AT&T, emails from Google accounts and Yahoo!, and all kinds of data that pertains to Kim's security clearance and briefings. They had badge records for "employees, contractors, and detailees" (people from other Departments of government working at State). Nineteen disks were mentioned as being transferred to the law firm, along with certain redacted materials and some classified filings. That is a lot of information.

It's fairly obvious the Justice Department was not just after someone who released one report to one reporter. It will take many more months to find out what this whole case is really about, and many more after that to discover all the details of others that were involved. It won't be about freedom of the press. It will be about National Security.

At the same time this was unfolding, we had Tim Cook, Apple's CEO and Lois Lerner, IRS employee, saying they had "done nothing wrong" to two different committees of Congress. Mr. Cook seemed to be on good ground, since he was saying his company just did what was allowed under existing tax laws. Many people may not be satisfied with that, but we are talking about what is legal and what is illegal. No surveys will be taken to find out whether people like Apple because they make money.

Ms. Lerner was in charge of offices in Cincinnati, that were looking into the tax exempt status of conservative groups. The Director of the IRS had already been removed by the President, so the old adage that things flow downhill, only works if the material is not warded off by a stone wall. The problems are flowing in both directions in the IRS, causing no end of confusion. The lessons of *The Informant* may apply here.

Apple was being accused of doing something that is sound business practice, and the IRS was being accused of doing something that was sound political practice in places like Chicago, when I lived there; many dead voters cast ballots during one of our elections. We have to leave it to the Justice Department to decide whether these things are criminal.

The Wall Street Journal reported a number of companies have, over the last few years, started to eliminate their overseas subsidiaries from their filings. They used the old excuse that there are so many of these places that they just become hard to keep up. It was too much work. This stretches my brain trying to imagine the exceedingly complex tasks required to keep a list of overseas subsidiaries current. They recognized that overseas subsidiaries could be trouble if they didn't actually manufacture anything and if they looked like tax havens for money that was only taxed if it came back to the U.S. Even though this was not illegal, in most circumstances, the Corporate Boards knew how it would look. In other words, as long as it stayed a secret, nobody would get the wrong idea about why these businesses were being created.

In the IRS we have a different situation. Having worked for the IRS for a short time, I can say it is a hated organization, and nothing would prevent me from saying that anyway, but I wouldn't have the personal exposure to it.

On the first anniversary of our marriage, my wife and I went around the corner to a beautiful high-rise hotel where we had a suite. They treat you better in a suite, and we had the bridal suite, so everyone thought we were on our honeymoon. They were really helpful and booked us into the packed Comedy Club without a prior reservation, even giving us a seat down front – which we declined. We had been to these places before.

The first comedian came out and did a warm up act asking people in the audience where they worked and commenting on those places from his experience. The spotlight eventually fell on us. "Who are you and where do you work?" he asked.

"My name is Dennis and I work for the Internal Revenue Service." He said nothing for too long a time and there were a few nervous laughs of the people around us who were waiting for the big comeback. It reminded me of the reaction we got at parties when someone asked where we worked. The most common response was "Oh."

"I pay my taxes", he said finally, and started looking for someone else to call on.

The couple at the table we had declined were called on next, and the young guy was ready, "Hi, my name is David and I work for the Defense Intelligence Agency", which he also knew nothing about. Being a Washington crowd, everyone there knew it, and it brought down the house. We felt sorry for the comic and had another drink.

The IRS will be clobbered by Committees and Hearings for many months to come, but it won't be because they did a number of things wrong. If they were doing some of the things they were accused of doing, they deserve it, but they were going to get blasted anyway. Washington hates them.

To make matters worse, they tried to keep something, already involved in an Inspector General (IG) investigation, from getting out. It is not possible, and everyone in Washington knows it. When things get to an IG, the leaders have already jumped off the cliff and are just looking for ways to avoid dying in the drop. We once gave the Chief Information Officer of the IRS a report on the types of fraud we expected from the first year of automated filing and he said, "Oh I heard about this" and passed it to a person to remove from his office. Everything that we said would happen did, but he "didn't know" about the findings and survived the fall during the investigations that followed.

To allow the current shenanigans to go on until an internal IG report was finished is beyond belief, but in Washington politics, it is accepted practice. The White House says it didn't want to interfere, with an on-going investigation. You remember that line from similar cases in previous administrations. They should have known the secret was out and cut their losses, ala David Letterman. They won't be the last government entity to carry on when confession, and redemption, would be better all around.

In May, 60 Minutes updated its story on the raid that killed Osama Bin Laden and produced the book *No Easy Day*, published by Penguin Books (USA) Inc. Part of the story now reads that George Neal, a Defense Department spokesman, says the author was "in material breach of his secrecy agreement", the first step in moving to legal action. The author still maintains that there is no classified information in it, but I once asked the Intelligence Community reviewers if they could stop the publication of a book that was written and sent to a publisher, without getting approval. They said, "No, but we can stop you from benefiting from it." This hardly seems like the best approach to take, but, on balance, it may be the only approach our country will accept. We could do much more, but may not be willing to live with what that might be.

We are learning this lessons again with Edward Snowden. His secrets come clearly marked as Really Big ones. It should be obvious that the keeping of secrets was important to business and government leaders, but we never know which secrets are the most important at any given time. We try to pretend that we want to be open, and share information with our best friends, business partners, and other countries, but we might be better off no doing that, without some thought.

Too many people are involved in saying what is worth protecting, and too many involved in inventing new things to protect. If we are going to be as free and open as we think we should be, then let's all start to think about what we really need to have as secrets. A few individuals in each company and each level of government can do that formally, but a mother's words to her children about respecting the rights of others can mean almost as much.

Dennis F. Poindexter

Since 2010, Dennis is a writer. His first book, *The Chinese Information War, Espionage, Cyberwar, Communications Control and Related Threats to United States Interests*, (McFarland Publishing, Inc.) was published in March 2013.

After thirty-two years of government service, including six as Director of Security and Information Assurance, Ballistic Missile Defense Organization, he worked in private industry where he was an industry member of the President's Critical infrastructure Protection Committee, a Staff Consultant to the US House of Representatives, and Director of Security Architecture at EDS.

He later served five years in the FBI, including two in Counter-Terrorism Operations.

He was a permanent faculty member of the Defense Security Institute and a two-time Chairman of the Computer Security Educators Association. He has presented papers five times at the Canadian IT Security Symposium in Ottawa, and spoken over three hundred times at industry and government functions in the United States.

144 Ellen Nakashima, *Confidential report lists U.S. weapons system designs compromised by Chinese cyberspies*, Washington Post, 27 May 2013

145 Associated Press, *Justice Department secretly obtained AP phone records*, May 13, 2013

146 Fox News *Obama orders Justice Department review after Fox News, AP phone records seized* : http://www.foxnews.com/politics/2013/05/23/obama-orders-doj-review-after-reporter-record-seizures/#ixzz2UOWqqzut

147 The Department of Justice letter to the law firm and its reply are found at http://www.fas.org/sgp/jud/kim/101311-discovery58.pdf

BIBLIOGRAPHY

Major Sources

David E. Sanger, "Confront and Conceal: Obama's Secret Wars and Surprising Use of American Power, (Broadway Paperbacks, New York, New York), 2012

David Von Drehle FBI's No. 2 Was 'Deep Throat', Mark Felt Ends 30-Year Mystery of The Post's Watergate Source, Washington Post, 1 June 2005

Dr. Mathew Levitt, *Iranian Terror Operations on American Soil*, Testimony before a joint hearing of the House Homeland Security Subcommittee on Counterterrorism and Intelligence and Subcommittee on Oversight, Investigations, and Management, October 26, 2011

Graham Allison, *The Commission on America's National Interests*, John F. Kennedy School of Government, Harvard University, July 2000, page 7-10

Joe Becker and Scott Shane, *Assessing Obama's Counterterrorism Record*, New York Times, 29 May 2012, accessed 6 Nov 2012

Kurt Eichenwald, *The Informant*, (Broadway Books, New York, New York) 2000.

Mandiant APT1, Exposing One of China's Cyber Espionage Units, Mandiant Corporation, report date 18 February 2013.

No Safe Haven, Iran's Global Assassination Campaign, Iran Human Rights Documentation Center, Appendix 1 "Chronological List of those Killed during the Islamic Republic of Iran's Global Assassination Campaign", May 2008

Symantec, *Internet Security Threat Report, 2013*, Symantec Corporation

The 9/11 Commission Report: Identifying and Preventing Terrorist Financing, 23 August 2004

U.S. District Court, Southern District of New York, Securities and Exchange Commission vs. Galleon Management LP, et. al. 02 September 2010

Verizon, *2013 Data Breach Investigations Report*, Verizon, May 2013.

China-North Korea Relations, Congressional Research Office

Other Sources

Aki J. Peritz, Eric Rosenbach, Published as a background memo in Confrontation or Collaboration Congress and the Intelligence Community, Belfer Center for Science and International Affairs, John F. Kennedy School of Government, Harvard University, July 2001

Catherine Herridge, Exclusive: Pentagon Attempts to Block Book on Afgan War,

Nicole Perlroth, Hackers in China Attacked the Times in the Last 4 Months, New York Times, 30 January, 2013

R. Jeffrey Smith and Joby Warrick, *Pakistani Scientist Khan describes Iranian efforts to buy nuclear bombs,* Washington Post, March 14, 2010, and Christopher Clary, *The A. Q. KHAN Network: Causes and Implications*, Naval Post Graduate School, December 2005

50 U.S.C. § 435b : US Code - Section 435B: Security Clearances

Adam Goldman, *U.S.: CIA thwarts new al-Qaida underwear bomb plot*, Denver Post, posted 05/07/2012

Al Qaeda Funding in Afghanistan, Global Security.Org.

Alexei Anishchuk, Suicide Bomber Kills 35 at Moscow's Biggest Airport, Reuters, 24 January 2011

Ali Aalaei, America Invents Act of 2011: Good or Bad for Small Businesses?, website accessed

American Civil Liberties Union, *Briefing Paper #4, Lie Detector Testing*, undated

Amit Agarwal, *We Love Microsoft Software Piracy in China: Bill Gates*, Digital Inspiration, 23July 2007

Annual Information Security Oversight Report to the President, 2010

Associated Press, *Cash-Strapped Al Qaeda Turns to Kidnapping and Ransom to pay Operational Costs*, Fox News, 19 June, 2011

Associated Press, Chechen Rebels Hurting for Money, September 2004

Associated Press, *Justice Department secretly obtained AP phone records*, May 13, 2013

Associated Press, *Seven Navy SEALS Reprimanded for Leaking Information*, Wall Street Journal, 8 November 2012

BBC *Afghanistan Profile*, 31 March 2013

BBC News, *'Anti-Semitic' French envoy under fire*, 20 December 2001

BBC News, *Al Qaeda Yemen Plane Bomb Plot Foiled by 'Insider"*, 08 May 2012

BBC News, *Enron at-a-glance*, 22 August 2002

BBC News, How Potent are North Korea's Threats? 2 April 2013

Bradley Graham, *Hackers Attack Via Chinese Web Sites*, Washington Post, 25 August 2005

Brendan McGarry, Army Set to Introduce Smartphones in Combat, Wired, 27 March 2013

Brian Ross, Richard Espisito, and Rhonda Schwartz, *Officials: More Al Qaeda Bombs Unaccounted for*, ABC Nightline, 7 May 2012

Carlos Tejada, *Many U.S. Companies in China Site Data Theft*, Wall Street Journal, Updated version 29 March 2013

Catherine J. Lanctot, Attorney-Client Relationships in Cyberspace: The Peril and the Promise, Duke University Law Library

China-North Korea Relations, Congressional Research Office, December 28, 2010, page 4

Chris Cuomo, *Rep. Anthony Weiner: 'The Picture Was of Me and I Sent It'*, 6 June 2011

Christie Nicholson, Keeping Secrets Weighs You Down, Literally, Scientific American, 29 April 2012

Christopher Drew, Stolen Data is Tracked to Hacking at Lockheed, New York Times, 3 June, 2011

Clyde Prestowitz, *America Needs a New Globalization Game*, Huffington Post 29 April 2012, online, accessed 11/05.2012

CNN Staff Writer, *Workers Exhuming Yasser Arafat's Body in Probe of Death*, 5 November 2012

Colin J. Zick, "Security and Privacy in 2011: How to stay a step ahead," (Jan. 2011), Used with permission.

Daily Mail on line, WikiLeaks cable 'led Iran to hang kick-boxer it claims was Israeli spy who assassinated nuclear scientist' 16 May 2012

Daniel Kadiec, *Enron: Who's Accountable?* Time Magazine, 13 January 2002

Daubert v. Merrell Dow Pharmaceuticals, 509 U.S. 579, 113 S.Ct. 2786, 125 L.Ed.2d 468 (1993)

David E. Sanger, *Obama Order Sped up Waves of Cyberattacks Against Iran*, New York Times, June1, 2012

David Von Drehle FBI's No. 2 Was 'Deep Throat', Mark Felt Ends 30-Year Mystery of The Post's Watergate Source, Washington Post, 1 June 2005

Debra Saunders, *Feinstein Takes On White House Leaks*, Real Clear Politics, 14 June 2012

Department of Defense Inspector General, *Requirements for the TRAILBLAZER and THINTHREAD Systems* (redacted), December 15, 2004 [Note: redacted here means there are one or two lines of text on a printed page and not much more].

Dirk Adriaensens, Boston on the Tigris, Iraq's Unreported Terror Event, Global Research, 23 April 2013

Dombey, Daniel, *CIA admits errors led to Afghanistan attack*, and Windren, Robert and Engel, Richard, NBC News

Dr. Mathew Levitt, *Iranian Terror Operations on American Soil*, Testimony before a joint hearing of the House Homeland Security Subcommittee on Counterterrorism and Intelligence and Subcommittee on Oversight, Investigations, and Management, October 26, 2011

Dylan Byers, *Broadwell's co-author to publish WaPo piece*, Politico, November 12, 2012

Ed O'Keefe, Court *Rebuffs FBI Polygraphs*, ABC News, 2 August (no year given)

EDS Settlement Orders, Order and Final Judgment Approving Proposed Settlement, 6 August 2008

Edward Pound and David Rogers, *An Israeli Contract With a U.S. Company Leads to Espionage*, Wall Street Journal, January 17, 1992.

Eichenwald, Kurt, The Informant, (Broadway Books, New York, New York) 2000.

Elinor Abreu, *Cyber Attacks Reveal Cracks in U.S. Defense*, PCWorld, 9 May 2001

Elise Labott, *Obama Authorized Covert Support for Syrian Rebels*, Sources Say, CNN, August 1, 2012

Ellen Nakashima, *Confidential report lists U.S. weapons system designs compromised by Chinese cyberspies*, Washington Post, 27 May 2013

Eric Schmitt, *American Strike is said to Kill Top Qaeda Leader*, New York Times, 31 May, 2010

Ewen MacAsKill, *Al Qaida (sic) Bomb Plot Thwarted by CIA*, The Guardian, 7 May 2012

Executive Office of the President, The Security Clearance Oversight Group, Consistent with Title III, of the Terrorist Reform and Terrorism Prevention Act, 2004, published February 2007

Executive Order 13292, Classified National Security Information, April 2009, page 1.

Fox News *Obama orders Justice Department review after Fox News, AP phone records seized*

Frederick W. Whately, Reagan, *National Security, and the First Amendment: Plugging Leaks by Shutting Off the Main*, 8 May,

1984, Copyright Cato Institute,(used by permission, Cato Institute)

Fundamental Classification Guidance Review, Information Security Oversight Office, 2012

Government Accountability Project, NSA Whistleblower Thomas Drake

Graham Allison, *The Commission on America's National Interests*, John F. Kennedy School of Government, Harvard University, July 2000, page 7-10.

Indictment, U.S. District Court, Southern District of Texas, 03/07/2002

Information Security Oversight Office, 20010 Report to the President, page 3.

James Adams and Douglas Frantz, *A Full Service Bank*, Pocket Books (New York, New York) April 1992, page 5-6.

James Bandler and Nicholas Varchaver, How Bernie Did It, CNN Money, April 30, 2009

James O`Shea and George Curry, *CIA's Shot at Media Backfires*, Chicago Tribune, June 01, 1986

Jamil Anderlini, *Quarter of US groups in China claim to be cyber attack victims*, Financial Times, 30-31 March 2013

Jeannie Whalen, Devlin Barrett, Peter Loftus, *Glaxco in $3 Billion Settlement*, Wall Street Journal, 3 July 2012

Jeff Green, Bloomberg News, *Sex-Scandal CEOs Spark Debate on What's Different in the C-Suite*, the San Francisco Chronicle, Nov 13 2012

Jennifer Waters, *Why ID Thieves Love Social Media*, Wall Street Journal, 25 March 2012

Jessica Ramirez, *Educating Elite Hackers*, The Daily Beast, Mar 10, 2010

Jill Dougherty, Moscow Metro Blast Kills 39, CNN, 6 February, 2004

Jim Dwyer, William K. Rashbaum and John Eligon, *Strauss-Kahn Prosecution Said to Be Near Collapse*, New York times, 20 June, 2011

Jim Dwyer, William K. Rashbaum, John Eligon, Strauss-Kahn Prosecution Said to Be Near Collapse, 30 June 2011

Joby Warrick, *Iran Bolsters Retaliation Capability in Persian Gulf, Experts Say*, Washington Post, 26 July 2012

Joe Becker and Scott Shane, *Assessing Obama's Counterterrorism Record*, New York Times, May 29, 2012

Joe Becker and Scott Shane, Secret 'Kill List' Proves a Test of Obama's Principles and Will, 29 May 2012

John Markoff and David E. Sanger, *In a Computer Worm, a Possible Biblical Clue*, New York times, September 29, 2010

Josh Ong, *US judge rules that Samsung was responsible for deleted emails in Apple patent suit*, The Next Web, 25 July 2012

Judicial Watch Website, accessed 30 October 2012, Judicial Watch Obtains DOD and CIA Records Detailing Meetings with bin Laden Raid Filmmakers

Julian Barnes & Jay Solomon, *Iran Fired on U.S. Drone before Vote*, Wall Street Journal, 9 November 2012

Julian E. Barnes, *Law Agencies Seek More Data From Cell Carriers*, Wall Street Journal, 9 July 2012

Kate Linebaugh, UTC Helped China Build First Military Attack Copter, Wall Street Journal, June 28, 2012

Katz, Marshall, and Banks, *Supreme Court Lets SOX Media Leaks Ruling Stand,* Sarbanes-Oxley Whistleblower Blog, 1 November 2011

Ken Dilanian and Brian Bennett, *Al Qaeda Bomb Plot was Foiled by Double Agent,* Los Angeles Times, 9 May 2012

Kevin Poulsen and Kim Zetter, *I Can't Believe What I'm Confessing to You': The Wikileaks Chats,* Wired, June 10, 2010

Kim Zetter, *Researchers Connect Flame to US-Israel Stuxnet Attack,* Wired, June 11, 2012

Krebs on Security, Who Else was Hit by the RSA Attackers, website accessed

Lawyers.com, Blackmail Costs More than it Pays, accessed 14 November 2012,

Matt Coker, *Monica Quan, Titans Basketball Coach, and Fiance Keith Lawrence Found Shot to Death,* OC Weekly, 5 Feb 2013

Matthew Fisher, Harper Moves for Presence in Straight of Hormuz with Regina Deployment, National Post, 3 September 2012

Matthew Levitt and Michael Jacobson, The Money Trail, Finding, Following and Freezing Terrorist Financing , November 2008

Michael Kelley, *BY THE NUMBERS: Why The Mexican Drug War Should Keep You Awake At Night, business Insider,* 18 June 2012

Nasir Habib, *Senior al Qaeda leader killed in Pakistan,* officials say, CNN, 10 December 2012

Nate Raymond, *DOJ Filings on $25 Billion Settlement Detail Whistleblower Claims,* Law.com, 15 March 2012

NBC News, *FBI Agent Sent Shirtless Photo to Kelley before email Investigation, Officials Say* 13 November 2012

Neal Underleider, *Hacked? Mandiant's Cyberattack Detectives want to know all about it,* FastCompany, 3 April 2013

Nelson d. Schwartz, *Facing Threat from Wikileaks, Bank Plays Defense,* New York Times, 2 January 2011

Nicolas Falliere, Liam O Murchu, and Eric Chien, *W32.Stuxnet Dossier,* February 2011 (this appears at version 1.4 and originated in 2010)

Nirmala Ganapathy, *India Launches 7 Satellites in One Go,* The Strait Times, February 26, 2013 and United Nations Report, *Satellite Debris,* June 2008.

Nirmalya Kumar, Louis W. Stern, James C. Anderson, *Conducting Interorganizational Research Using Key Informants,* The Academy of Management Journal, Vol. 36, No. 6 (Dec., 1993), pp. 1633-1651

No Safe Haven, Iran's Global Assassination Campaign, Iran Human Rights Documentation Center, Appendix 1 "Chronological List of those Killed during the Islamic Republic of Iran's Global Assassination Campaign", May 2008

NOVA, *Investigating 9/11,* Public Broadcasting, 01 January 2009

Open Secrets, Wikileaks, War and American Diplomacy (Grove Press, New York, New York*),* Page 22.

Pam Benson, *CNN Fact check: Is al Qaeda's Core Decimated or is Group Growing,* CNN, 23 October 2012

Pascal Rossignol, *France's Strauss Kahn under Investigation in Pimping Case,* Reuters, 26 March 2012

Peter Bergen, *Who Really Killed Bin Laden?,* CNN World, updated 27 March 2013

Peter Loftus, *Whistleblower's Long Journey,* Wall Street Journal, 28 October 2010

Reforming China's Gulags, BBC News, 17 March 2013

Reuters, *Iran Airs 'Confessions' in Killings of Nuclear Scientists*, 6 August 2012

Richard A. Oppel Jr., Mark Mazzetti and Souad Mekhennet, *Attacker in Afghanistan was a Double Agent* Published: January 4, 2010

Russel D. Hoffman, An Interview with Phil Zimmerman, High Tech Today, 2 February 1996

Sara Forden, Google Said to Face Fine by U.S. over Apple Safari Breach, 9 August 2012, Bloomberg Technology

Sascha Fahl, Marian Harbach, Thomas Muders, Matthew Smith, Lars Baumgärtner, Bernd Freisleben, *Why Eve and Mallory Love Android: An Analysis of Android SSL (In)Security*, University of Hanover, copy write CCS'12, October 16–18, 2012, Raleigh, North Carolina, USA, September 10, 2010

Sharon Waxman, *The Sex Parties of France's DSK: 'Eyes Wide Shut' Comes to Life*, The Wrap, 15 October 2012

Sherry Sontag, Christopher Drew, *Blind Man's Bluff*, Harper Collins Publisher (New York, New York), page 416.

Siobhan Gorman, *Drone Victims' Kin Sue Government*, Wall Street Journal, July 18, 2012

Siobhan Gorman, *Iran Renews Internet Attacks on U.S. Banks*, Wall Street Journal, 17 October 2012, accessed 30 October 2012

Staff Writer (unnamed), *John Edwards*, New York Times, updated 13 June 2012

Steven Aftergood, *Court Rebuffs FBI Censorship of Manuscript*, Federation of American Scientists.

Susan Pulliam and Chad Bray, *Trader Draws Record Sentence*, Wall Street Journal, 13 October 2011

Svetlana Savranskaya, (ed), Volume II: Afghanistan: Lessons from the Last War, The National Security Archive

Symantec, *Internet Security Threat Report, 2013*, Symantec Corporation, page 4.

TASS, *London Coroner's Court to probe into Berezovsky's involvement in Litvinenko death*, 3 Nov 2012

The 9/11 Commission Report: Identifying and Preventing Terrorist Financing, 23 August 2004

The Leaky Corporation, The Economist, 24 February 2011

The List: The Political Assassinations of 2006, Foreign Policy, 27 November 2006

The World Intellectual Property Organization, *2011 Intellectual Property Indicators*, 2011, page 20.

Thom Shanker, Eric Schmitt & David E. Sanger, *U.S. Adds Forces to Persian Gulf, a Signal to Iran*, New York Times, July 3, 2012

Title 50 USC § 413B - PRESIDENTIAL APPROVAL AND REPORTING OF COVERT ACTIONS

Tom Frijins, *Keeping Secrets*, Quality, Quantity and Consequences, 13 December 2004

Tony Capaccio, *Pentagon Continues Use of China Satellite in New Lease*, Bloomburg, 15 May 2013.

U.S. District Court, Southern District of New York, Securities and Exchange Commission vs. Galleon Management LP, et. al. 02 September 2010

Uniform Trade Secrets Act, Legal Information Institute, Cornell University

Washington Post, Monday, May 7, 2001; Page A02

Washington Wire Staff Writer, *Timeline of the Petraeus Scandal*, Wall Street Journal, 13 November 2012

William Lee Adams, *Is This the Real Thing? Coca-Cola's Secret Formula 'Discovered'*, Time Newsfeed, 15 February 2013